THE
Sugar Cube

THE

Sugar Cube

50 Deliciously Twisted Treats from
the Sweetest Little Food Cart on the Planet

by Kir Jensen
with Danielle Centoni

photographs by Lisa Warninger

CHRONICLE BOOKS
SAN FRANCISCO

Library of Congress Cataloging-in-Publication Data available.

ISBN 978-1-4521-0126-2

Manufactured in China

FSC
www.fsc.org

MIX
Paper from
responsible sources
FSC® C104723

Designed and illustrated by *Cat Grishaver*
Prop styling by *Chelsea Fuss*
Food styling by *Kir Jensen*

10 9 8 7 6 5 4 3 2 1

Chronicle Books LLC
680 Second Street
San Francisco, California 94107
www.chroniclebooks.com

This book is dedicated to one very inspiring woman—my mom. Thank you for teaching me to be an expert fruit fondler, lover of good food, feeder of the masses, and diner by candlelight.

Kir Jensen is chef/owner of The Sugar Cube. She lives in Portland, Oregon. This is her first book.

Danielle Centoni is a food writer whose work has appeared in the *Oregonian*, the *New York Times*, *Fine Cooking*, *Sunset*, and *Saveur* and is coauthor of *Mother's Best: Comfort Food That Takes You Home Again*. She lives in Portland, Oregon.

Lisa Warninger is a photographer specializing in lifestyle, fashion, and food. She lives in the Northwest.

Chronicle Books publishes distinctive books and gifts. From award-winning children's titles, best-selling cookbooks, and eclectic pop culture to acclaimed works of art and design, stationery, and journals, we craft publishing that's instantly recognizable for its spirit and creativity. Enjoy our publishing and become part of our community at www.chroniclebooks.com.

Contents

Introduction

I remember it like it was yesterday, the moment that sparked my lust for all things sweet. I'm about six years old, standing patiently next to my mom in the kitchen, our favorite room in the house. I loved how its soft lighting just seemed to glow and how the warm yellow hue of the walls and the sky-blue–tiled backsplash reminded me of the sunniest summer days. For my mom, a native Swiss, the colors were a reminder of her homeland.

I'm rapt, watching as my mom's strong hands wrangle the old workhorse hand mixer, the beaters clattering against the faded yellow milk-glass mixing bowl as she beats the yellow cake mix into a thick, fluffy cloud. As it whines like a mini motorboat, nearly drowning out the soft rock playing in the background, cake-mix dust wafts toward my crinkling nose. I can almost taste the sweet, creamy batter, but between my mom's watchful eye and the ferocious blades of the mixer, I don't dare dip in a finger.

The motor stops.

"Here," my mom softly whispers.

Finally! Time almost seems to stand still as my mom lovingly hands me a batter-coated beater. As the not-so-natural yellow goo drips all over my tiny fingers and feet, I quickly set to work, trying to lap up every drop.

"You know, you'll get vurms if you eat too much of the raw batter," my mom says almost halfheartedly in her thick Swiss accent. She was big on old wives' tales and Old World superstitions, but her fear was no match for the pleasure she got from looking at the joy on my face. I knew I'd soon be licking the bowl, too.

And that's when something deep within me just clicked. That's when I realized that food and love were deliciously, beautifully intertwined. When she handed me that beater, my mother taught me not only to love food but to love sharing it with others, too.

Twenty-seven years later, I've turned that lesson into my career.

Looking back, it seems almost inevitable that I would end up attending the Baking and Pastry Program at the Cooking and Hospitality Institute of Chicago, near my hometown. Soon thereafter I began working at Trio, a four-star restaurant in Chicago, where I trained under renowned pastry chef Della Gossett, whose creativity and skill helped shape the way I bake.

When I got the itch to head west, I moved to Portland and spent several years working at acclaimed bakeries and restaurants like Florio, Genoa, Noble Rot, and Clarklewis. Finally, in

2008, I decided it was time to pave my own way. With limited funds but enthusiasm to spare, I opened The Sugar Cube food cart—my own space—where I could grow as a baker, define my own style, and connect with my customers in a personal way that's usually not possible in a commercial kitchen. Not only would I get to bake their treats, but I also would be able to hand them out personally and see the pleasure on their faces as they took a bite. Finally, I'd be able to really spread my own brand of sugar love.

My cart was one of the first in the city to offer something beyond the usual taco-truck fare and certainly the first to specialize in desserts, so word quickly spread. Portlanders were hungry for my deliciously twisted takes on cupcakes and cookies, puddings and drinks, all made with high-quality, locally sourced ingredients. Then journalists started calling, photographers started snapping my picture, and soon my little cart was getting ink in publications like the *New York Times*, *Los Angeles Times*, *Sunset* magazine, and *Travel + Leisure*.

It always seemed to surprise people that I baked everything out of the cart. It wasn't just a tiny retail space; it was also my workspace. This got me thinking: If I can make ganache-filled brownies, salted caramel-topped cupcakes, and brown-butter tarts out of an eight-by-fourteen-foot food cart, then anyone can, no matter how tiny the kitchen. And that's how this book was born. I don't have space for big, fancy equipment, acres of tools, or miles of shelves with luxurious staples. But I don't need them, and neither do you.

So this book is for all you dessert hounds out there who think you can't bake because you don't have the right kitchen, the right equipment, or the right recipes. That's B.S. If you can follow a recipe and have a little patience, you can become a whisk-wielding badass—and you don't need a six burner Wolf range to do it. I'll tell you how to outfit your tiny kitchen or baking area and work efficiently within it, how to pick the best ingredients, and how to turn those ingredients into kick-ass desserts.

Don't forget that baking is something that is done with love and care, and making family recipes is one of the best ways to remember and honor the ones you love and miss. If you're lucky enough to have a big box of old recipes from your mom or grandma, cherish them—and use them. Let this book encourage you to fire up your oven and remember your roots.

So turn the page and don your apron. There's nothing terribly difficult or labor intensive in here, because that's not what I'm about. But you will find plenty of chances to get your hands dirty with a little butter and sugar—and plenty of delicious reasons to share the sugar love.

XoXo!
Kir

1

TRADE
SECRETS

I really do love my tiny pink food cart. I love that it gives me my own space, outside of my house, where I can craft tasty little treats for the very appreciative food lovers in my town. I love that I can afford to own it without signing my life over to a bank or charging my customers outrageous prices. And I love that I don't have to share it with anyone. It's all mine. There's no one else there bumping into me or running off with my pans. It's my domain, like an artist's studio, where I have space to create.

My cart has all of these great things going for it *because* it's small. But "small" also means "challenging." First of all, weathering the seasons can be a serious problem. Unlike an actual building with, say, central heat, air-conditioning, and insulation, my cart is out there in the elements. In winter, it's so cold I can't get my butter to soften. In summer, it's so hot that turning on the oven feels like an act of insanity. An even more constant issue is limited workspace. The cart is just eight feet wide and fourteen feet long. Tiny, right? Well, once you put the oven, racks, sink, and counter in there, it feels a whole lot smaller.

To cope, I follow several major rules that, really, everyone should follow no matter what size his or her kitchen.

FIRST: Don't be a slob.

This is the rule they beat into you at cooking school: Work clean, and your product turns out clean. No matter how slovenly you may be in the rest of your life, you can't be a slob in the kitchen. Not only is it unsanitary, but you're also more likely to make mistakes. This is especially important when your kitchen is minuscule. I absolutely must clean up as I go, or I literally won't have room to cook.

SECOND: Be prepared.

Before I do any mixing I get my *mise en place* ready: I measure out all my ingredients and have them prepped. This way I can make sure that I have everything I need and that it's all at the right temperature. There's no room to stop midrecipe and put everything aside for a while. And there's no room in my cart, or my budget, for mistakes. In baking you usually get only one chance to add your ingredient at the right time. If you miss it, you're screwed.

THIRD: Stay focused.

If I have several things on my baking agenda, I don't have room to start one recipe until the other is finished. As much as I want to multitask, I can't. And that's a good thing because it means I can focus properly on that particular recipe and am less likely to forget a step or make a mistake.

FOURTH: Master your domain.

Making sure that I have all the tools I need and that they're all organized in a logical way keeps me baking efficiently—and also saves me from going nuts. No one wants to crisscross the kitchen dozens of times to fetch this and grab that when cooking. It's exhausting, annoying, and can create problems when making things that rely on crucial timing.

No matter what size your kitchen, if you love to bake, you should try to create a baking station. This could be a corner of the kitchen where there's a good smooth work surface, an outlet for your mixer or food processor, and a cupboard at least a portion of which you can dedicate to common dry ingredients like flour, sugar, and baking spices. If there's a drawer, reserve it for your whisks and spatulas, or get an extra utensil crock just for these baking tools so they're all in one place.

Everyone's kitchen is different, and only you can organize yours in a way that works best for you. Just think about how and when and where you typically use your tools, and let that be your guide. If you have a large kitchen and the stove is far from the area where you typically mix your doughs, you might need two sets of certain tools, like whisks and spatulas, so one can stay near the stove and one can stay near the baking station. It's not overkill if it means you'll be able to bake more efficiently and enjoy doing it. As for which tools and ingredients you need, turn the page to get my picks for the absolute essentials no kitchen—no matter how small—should be without.

Airtight containers: Sturdy plastic airtight containers in all sizes are essential for keeping your treats from going stale or getting freezer burn.

Blender: Sometimes food processors fail where blenders succeed, especially when it comes to smoothies, milk shakes, and recipes with lots of liquid. Sometimes they do a better job at puréeing, too.

Brush: You'll need at least one pastry brush for brushing the tops of cupcakes with flavorful syrups or brushing piecrusts with cream or egg wash. I prefer natural-bristle brushes, because they're gentler on your delicate treats and they can soak up and distribute liquid better. Be sure to clean them well and air-dry thoroughly after use, so they don't retain flavors and odors or mildew.

Cheesecloth: This loose-mesh fabric is great for lining sieves and colanders to strain out tiny particles. It is available in small packages at kitchen supply stores.

Colander and fine-mesh sieve:
A colander with large holes is useful for rinsing fruits. A fine-mesh sieve or strainer is essential for straining out small particles to make the smoothest custards and curds. You can also use it as a sifter, which is what I do, thereby eliminating the need for another piece of kitchen equipment. To help push the dry ingredients through, just stir them with a whisk.

Cooling racks: These give you a place to put your just-baked cookies, so they can stop cooking and start cooling. Racks that stack on top of each other are great because they use up less counter space. It's also good to have a metal heat-safe rectangular rack that can fit on a rimmed baking sheet for making things like candied bacon; it lets the air circulate for even cooking and allows the fat to drip off.

Food processor: There are so many uses for food processors, from making biscuits and pie dough to grinding nuts into flour. No kitchen should be without one. If you ask me, Cuisinart is best. Get one with the biggest capacity you can—at least 9 cups but 14 cups is even better—so it has plenty of room to handle any recipe.

Graters: Rasp-style graters (Microplane is my choice) are the best. They enable you to remove the flavorful zest on citrus without digging into the pith, they easily grate nutmeg, and they shred the tough fibers of ginger like nobody's business. Don't bother getting a whole set; you need just two. Get the "classic" grater for most jobs, like grating ginger or chocolate, and one with slightly smaller holes for more delicate jobs, like zesting.

Ice-cream maker: Homemade ice creams and sorbets are such wonderful treats, but if you don't have an ice-cream maker, you'll be shut out of making this whole category of desserts. You don't have to spend top dollar on a fancy professional model. The Cuisinart ice-cream maker is a solid, affordable, no-fail choice. KitchenAid also makes a special bowl and attachment for its stand mixers.

Ice-cream scoops:

I use a 1-ounce (2-tablespoon) size for most drop cookies and a 2-ounce (1/4-cup) size for muffin and cupcake batter. I'm a huge fan of ice-cream scoops for portioning out cookie dough, truffles, and even cupcake and muffin batter. With little effort on your part, they enable you to be precise, so everything bakes at the same rate and looks uniform and professional. You can get half a dozen sizes at most restaurant supply stores.

Kitchen scissors:

Keep a separate pair of sharp scissors just for kitchen tasks like trimming the edges of pastry or snipping fresh herbs. Those dirty, gummed-up scissors you use for opening packages don't belong near your desserts.

Knives:

Invest in high-quality knives with high-carbon steel blades that run through the length of the handle, known as "full tang." Try them out. Hold them in your hand. See which knife feels good to you because it'll be like an extension of your hand. You'll need an **8- or 10-inch chef's knife** for most jobs. A **serrated bread knife** is essential for cutting through foods that are prone to squishing, like bread and tomatoes, and will make it easier to cut cakes into horizontal layers. It is also great for chopping chocolate. A **small paring knife** is handy for detail work. Store your knives in a knife block or on a magnetic strip. If you leave them loose in a drawer you run the risk of ruining the blade—and cutting yourself when reaching into the drawer. Get them professionally sharpened every few months, or invest in a Chef's Choice knife-sharpening machine, which takes the guesswork out of it.

Ladles:

They're not just for soup. Get a set in varying volumes from a restaurant supply store and use them to portion out batter, ladle custard into ramekins, stir cream into risotto, etc.

Marble slab:

You can get away with not having one of these, but they really are useful for keeping dough cold when rolling it out. If your kitchen or baking area doesn't have a good surface for rolling out dough (maybe you have a tile countertop or old, warped linoleum), you'll need a large, smooth surface of some sort to put on top, so you might as well make it marble! If you can't afford it, then get a large wooden cutting board. Whatever you choose, make sure it's at least 18 inches square so it can accommodate any recipe.

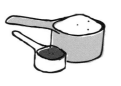

Measuring cups (dry):

These are made to be filled all the way, so you can scrape a metal spatula across the top to level it off for an accurate measure. Dry cup sizes should include 1/4 cup, 1/3 cup, 1/2 cup, and 1 cup. It's very handy to have two sets.

Measuring cups (liquid):

Liquid cups have a pour spout and plenty of extra room at the top so you can measure accurately without spilling a drop. Go for glass because it's easy to clean, see-through, and microwave safe. You'll need two or three in the 1-cup size (it's really very convenient having more than one). Then you'll need 2-cup, 4-cup, and 8-cup sizes. (The 8-cup can also double as a mixing bowl.)

Measuring spoons:

Choose metal, and, if you can, buy oblong instead of round, so they fit into narrow spaces like spice jars. Make sure the measurements are etched instead of printed on, so they won't rub off over time. The set should include: 1 tablespoon, 1 teaspoon, 1/2 teaspoon, 1/4 teaspoon, and 1/8 teaspoon.

Mixing bowls: You'll find a million uses for a set of nesting metal bowls. Restaurant supply stores stock stainless-steel bowls in all sizes, from tiny to massive. They're great for mixing, serving, holding hot mixtures that need to cool quickly (the metal transfers heat well), and functioning as a double boiler (just set the bowl over a pot of simmering water). Get them in a variety of sizes.

Parchment paper/ Silpat: Both parchment paper and Silpat provide a nonstick surface for baking cookies, preparing candies, or flash-freezing dollops of things like cookie dough. Parchment isn't reusable, but the good thing about it is you can cut it to fit, making it just right for lining cake pans or fitting into pie shells for blind baking. Rolls of parchment can be quite pricey at the supermarket. If you find yourself using it a lot, order a box of precut sheets (in the half-sheet size) from a restaurant supply store. It might seem expensive at first, but you'll end up with an almost lifetime supply. Silpats are reusable silicone sheets. You can find them at cookware stores. I love that they're reusable and incredibly nonstick.

Pastry bag with tips: You don't have to go bananas getting every pastry tip under the sun (and, believe me, there are a lot of them). But you should have at least one or two pastry bags plus a round tip and a star tip, preferably in small, medium, and large widths. Use them to put a decorative border on cakes, fill cream puffs, or pipe ultrasoft doughs.

Pastry blender: These are great for cutting butter into flour for biscuits and pie crusts, but a food processor does an even better job. If you have a processor, you can skip this.

Peeler: Like your knives, your peeler should have a sharp blade to make removing peels fast, easy, and safe. Make sure the handle is comfortable and allows for a firm grip.

Pepper grinder: Freshly ground pepper is so much more complex and aromatic than preground. It's almost like they're unrelated. You won't use it much in desserts, but sometimes a crack of black pepper can add depth when you least expect it. And for the love of God, please use freshly ground pepper in your savory ingredients.

Rolling pin: For rolling out pie dough, crushing cookies or crackers into crumbs, or beating butter to soften it up. Just get a plain wood one. Don't be tempted by other materials at the kitchen store.

Scale (digital): Everyone measures dry ingredients differently. Some spoon it into the cup, some use the cup as a scoop, and this can result in wildly different results. I prefer the "spoon-and-sweep" method, as do most professional chefs, and the recipes in this book were all made using that technique. Still, when in doubt, measuring these things by weight is the only way to ensure accuracy. Many cookbooks, especially newer ones, recognize this fact and offer weight measurements. So invest in a well-made digital scale that can measure both ounces and grams.

Spatula (rigid), a.k.a. pancake turner: Whether you choose metal or plastic, be sure you get one thin enough to slip under your just-baked cookies without wrecking them.

Spatulas (offset metal): A long, thin, metal spatula with an offset handle makes it easy to frost cakes or spread mixtures evenly and efficiently. Get a big one and a small one. I especially love my small offset and use it every chance I get.

Spatulas (flexible rubber): You'll need a couple of these in big and small sizes for scraping down your mixing bowl, folding ingredients, etc. To be on the safe side, make sure they're heat-proof silicone, which can withstand temperatures up to 500°F, so you can use them to cook with, too.

Spice grinder: The blade coffee grinders sold in most kitchen supply stores can double as electric spice mills, but be sure to reserve it just for spices (or your morning cup of coffee might taste like cloves and vice versa). Grinding whole spices gives you the freshest possible flavor. Make sure to wipe out the grinder with a damp cloth between grindings, or one spice will taste like the other.

Squeeze bottle: Plastic squeeze bottles with a narrow nozzle are great for piping decorative drizzles and swirls on your treats. You can get them cheap at restaurant supply stores, but these days most kitchen stores have them, too.

Stand mixer (preferably KitchenAid): More powerful than a handheld mixer, this makes whipping up fluffy cake batter and sturdy cookie dough effortless. There's really no substitute. Make sure you have the whisk, paddle, and dough hook attachments.

Thermometers: An oven running too hot or too cold can ruin a recipe, so get an oven thermometer to make sure your oven temp is spot on. You should also have a deep-frying/candy thermometer—you really don't want to guess with stuff like that. The old-school glass thermometers work just fine. If you want something easier to read, get a digital one.

Timer: Even if your oven or microwave has one, you'll need a separate timer when you're trying to keep track of two things at once. In my early days of baking, I would have three to four timers attached to me at all times.

Tongs: Tongs are so useful they're like having a pair of heat-proof hands. You can use them for all sorts of things, like turning donuts when deep frying. Get a pair that locks, so it's easier to store.

Whisks: Get a good sturdy whisk or two (it helps to have one large and one small) for blending ingredients or beating whipped cream or egg whites when you don't want to haul out the mixer.

Wooden spoons: They're cheap, don't scratch cookware, and can take a fair amount of heat. They're also the best way to tell if a sauce or custard has thickened properly because they allow the mixture to cling a bit.

Baking dishes: Essential sizes are 4-ounce ramekins (get at least eight); square 8-by-8-inch and rectangular 9-by-13-inch. I prefer Pyrex glass because it performs well for almost any use, and you can use it for layered creations like the Aric-A-Strata (page 25) and Donut-Misu (page 94). A metal 9-by-13-inch pan is also useful as a water bath for baking delicate custards.

Baking sheets: Rimmed baking sheets are serious workhorses, so be sure to have a bunch on hand. The most versatile size is a half sheet (18 by 13 inches). But you should have a quarter sheet, too, which is 9 by 13 inches. Make sure to get good, sturdy, heavy baking sheets in light metal. Good kitchenware stores will have them, but you can find them cheaper at a restaurant supply store.

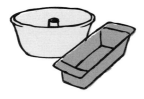

Cake pans: Round 8- or 9-inch pans are the most versatile standard sizes. Metal is always best. You should also have a 4-cup Bundt pan (for the "Passions" Breakfast Bundt Cake on page 35) and a 9-cup Bundt pan for bigger recipes; a 9-inch springform pan (which allows you to remove the sides for things like cheesecake); and a 10-inch tube pan with a removable bottom (for things like angel food cake).

Loaf pans: Standard loaf pans are usually 9 inches long, 5 inches wide, and 3 inches deep. Be sure to have two on hand in either glass or light-colored metal (dark metal retains more heat and can lead to overbaking) for loaf cakes and quick breads. I also love the elegant shape of a long Pullman loaf pan for things like the Le Almond (page 81) and highly recommend getting one.

Muffin pans: Make sure that each cup has a 1/2-cup capacity and that the metal is light, not dark (to prevent overbaking). A lot of cupcake and muffin recipes yield more than a dozen, so get at least two pans. Don't bother with nonstick (which gets scratched up easily), since you'll almost always be using muffin cup liners. I also like whoopie pie pans for baking some cookies or tea cakes, like the Hazelnibbies (page 59).

Pie pans: Most pie recipes call for a 9-inch pie dish. You can get glass or metal (I prefer glass so you can see the bottom to check how the crust is browning), but make sure you get a few in different depths. For a "normal" size pie, you want a depth of 1 1/2 inches. For a "deep-dish" pie, the pan will need to be 2 inches deep. A 1/2-inch difference may not seem like much, but the difference in volume is 3 cups. So if you don't use the pie dish with the right depth, you might end up with way too much or way too little filling.

Pots and pans: First, a note about metal—Aluminum and copper are great heat conductors, but they will react with acidic ingredients and may give your food a metallic taste. Copper is also very expensive and prone to tarnishing. Stainless steel won't react, but it doesn't conduct heat as well. That means the most versatile pans are anodized aluminum, stainless steel with an aluminum or copper core (my preference), or aluminum lined with stainless steel. No matter what brand you buy, make sure the cookware has a heavy bottom to keep things from burning and scorching. Recommended sizes are 8-inch, 10-inch, and 14-inch sauté pans, and 2-quart and 4-quart saucepans with lids. Make sure one of the saucepans is deep enough for making things that can bubble up, like caramel. I also think it's important to have at least one cast-iron skillet (9- or 10-inch). When seasoned properly they're nonstick, conduct heat evenly, retain heat very well, and can go in the oven. You can use them for just about anything—and they're great for baking cornbread or tarte Tatins.

Tart pans: Metal tart pans with a removable bottom are essential for fruit tarts and quiches, which rely on a pretty fluted crust. Get at least a 9-inch round, but 8-inch and 10-inch are also commonly used. A 4-by-13-inch rectangular tart pan is one of my favorite shapes and essential for the Raspberry–Brown Butter–Crème Fraîche Tart (page 69), so get one of those, too.

⚡ Pantry Staples ⚡

Now that you've got your baking domain properly set up, you need to stock your baking pantry. Having the most common ingredients on hand means you can make something awesome on the spur of the moment. But it's very important to choose your ingredients wisely; they're the building blocks of your desserts, after all. If they don't taste good, your dessert won't taste good, and your time, effort, and money will be wasted (plus your friends will be pissed they wasted their calories on it). As any chef will tell you, part of being a good cook is being a good shopper. So take time to choose your ingredients with care and spend a few extra pennies to get the best quality possible.

Butter: Although I love salt and sprinkle it liberally on my desserts to bring out and support the other flavors, I always bake with unsalted butter. Every butter producer adds different amounts of salt to their salted butter, making it harder to control the saltiness of the finished product. Also, salt is a preservative, so salted butter often isn't as fresh-from-the-dairy as unsalted butter. When choosing unsalted butter for baking, look for European-style butters, which have a higher fat content (and less water) and are often cultured so they have the slightest hint of tang. Some of my faves are Crèmerie Classic and Plugrá.

Chocolate: There is so much wonderful, interesting, nuanced chocolate out there that it would be a crime to settle for the cheap stuff in your desserts. For milk chocolate, make sure it's at least 41 percent cacao and comes from a quality producer, so it'll taste like more than just milk and sugar. For semisweet and bittersweet chocolate, the higher the percentage of cacao, the more intense and less sweet the flavor will be. My target range is 69 to 74 percent. For cocoa powder, darker is better in my book, so look for cocoa powder labeled Dutch process, European, dark, or extra-brut. In terms of producers, Callebaut is a good workhorse brand from Belgium. Valrhona, Scharffen Berger, and Green & Black's are also widely distributed brands with an emphasis on quality. There are a lot of smaller producers doing amazing stuff, too, so look around online or at a chocolate retailer like Cacao in Portland to find something new. For more on chocolate, read the sidebar on page 47.

Dairy: Sour cream, cream cheese, milk . . . if you're going to bake with them, you need to get the full-fat stuff. Fat equals flavor (I repeat: *Fat equals flavor!*), so don't skimp and use low-fat or non-fat. The few extra calories you save will be to the detriment of your dessert.

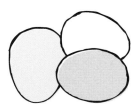

Eggs: I almost always use large eggs because they have just the right volume and the perfect ratio of yolk to white. If I specify extra-large, it's because the recipe relies on a slightly higher volume, so don't substitute. Although there's technically no difference in flavor between brown and white eggs (it's just the breed of hen that makes the egg shells a different color), there is a huge difference between store-bought and farm-fresh eggs. Farm-fresh eggs have darker orange yolks and more flavor—perfect for custards and ice cream bases—because the hens eat a more varied diet. They're also much fresher, usually just a couple days past being laid. You can tell because the yolks and whites look perky rather than runny. Heck, build your own coop if you have the space, and raise some chickens yourself! When I do have to buy eggs at the store rather than the farmers' market, I prefer hormone-free, locally raised eggs (like Stiebrs Farms). Local means they'll be fresher, so they'll perform better and taste better.

Flour: It's one of the most basic elements of pastry, so make sure it's the best. I use unbleached all-purpose flour for almost everything and typically reach for Oregon-produced Bob's Red Mill or Shepherd's Grain (which is also sustainably grown by a cooperative of small family farms in Oregon). King Arthur is also a good brand. Other flours I use for added flavor and texture, such as wheat, graham, nut, and buckwheat, tend to go rancid quickly, so store them in the freezer.

Fruit: You've heard it hundreds of times from hundreds of sources, but I'll say it, too: Buy your fruit in season, preferably from a local source. It *will* taste better, no doubt about it. Still, you shouldn't just blindly buy something just because it fits those two criteria. Think about it: If you had to choose between making a dessert with ripe, juicy, bursting-with-flavor strawberries and making one with dry, tasteless (but pretty!) strawberries, which would you pick? Stupid question, right? Not necessarily, because all too often people pick fruit based on how it looks (or the price per pound) without taking time to really hold it, examine it, smell it, ask for a taste. Those who don't really know what they're getting will very often end up with something sadly inferior. So be choosy. Be critical. Be forthright enough to ask for a taste—any good produce monger will be more than happy to geek out with you about produce and let you sample his or her goods.

Honey: There's no sense getting cheap, plain honey. It'll just taste sweet and one-dimensional, so you might as well use granulated sugar. If you're going to bake with honey, get something flavorful and unprocessed, so the nuances haven't been cooked out. I love going to farmers' markets to get local honey in a variety of flavors. I absolutely love meadowfoam because it has such a strong vanilla taste with complex pine undertones. Other good, flavorful honeys include lavender, wildflower, chestnut, and, if you like it really strong, buckwheat.

Nuts: Almonds, pecans, and hazelnuts are my favorite nuts to bake with. I keep them in the freezer so they stay as fresh as possible. There's a big difference in flavor between the mass-produced bags of nuts at the supermarket and farm-fresh nuts purchased from the source. If you can't get nuts at the farmers' market, look around online. Lots of farms sell their nuts directly to consumers through their Web sites.

Olive oil: There's neutral, inexpensive extra-virgin olive oil for sautéing, and then there's super-flavorful, cold-pressed, extra-virgin olive oil for drizzling. You need both. Not just one or the other. *Both.* Drizzle-worthy olive oil is pricey, but a little goes a long way. Some oils are burn-your-throat spicy and grassy, but I prefer something a touch milder and fruitier to use with chocolate and other sweets. Always sniff and taste your oil before using. If it smells musty, soapy, or acrid, it's gone rancid and will taste awful.

Salt: I use sea salt for everything because it comes in so many flavors, colors, and textures. When I'm adding salt to a batter, I usually use something fine grained, so it fits into measuring spoons better. For finishing salts, the sky's the limit, but I generally aim for something delicately flaky, like fleur de sel or Maldon. They add texture without being too coarse. For more on salt see page 122.

Spices: Ground spices lose their mojo pretty darn quick. They might look fine, but the flavors start to fade at six months and just get fainter and dustier as time goes on. One of the best options, though it requires a bit more patience, is to grind whole spices yourself in a spice grinder. Nutmeg, for sure, is one spice that I always use freshly ground, and you don't need a spice grinder to do it. Just grate the whole nutmeg on a Microplane until you have what you need for the recipe. If you are going to buy preground spices, buy smaller amounts so you can use them up before they lose their flavor. Places like Penzeys and The Spice House source the highest-quality spices, and you can order from them online. You can also check out the bulk section at your supermarket and buy smaller amounts that you'll use up fast. (Make sure it's a store with high turnover, so the bulk spices aren't old to begin with.)

Sugar: I prefer cane sugar over beet sugar, so C&H is my go-to brand. I use C&H's superfine "baker's" sugar instead of regular granulated sugar because it dissolves faster and therefore incorporates more quickly than regular granulated sugar. It also looks extra pretty when sprinkled on cookies, cakes, and pies. When I need brown sugar, I often reach for C&H "dark" brown, which is really as light as I like to go. If I need truly dark brown sugar, I get muscovado (a lot of supermarkets carry small bags of this on the baking aisle), which is almost chocolate brown because of its high molasses content.

Vanilla: There's a common theme in most of my recipes: Vanilla appears in almost all of them. Vanilla rounds out the rough edges of other flavors and adds depth. Although it can certainly stand on its own, it's an important supporting player, too. I always use high-quality pure vanilla extract from Penzeys or The Spice House because the flavor is more intense, nuanced, and I can select the variety of bean used, from Mexican to Tahitian. Whatever you do, don't get a cheap version that's mostly alcohol and water spiked with additives, or an imitation extract.

Sometimes extract isn't enough and you need the intensity of flavor that only comes from actual vanilla beans. So stock up on plump, fresh, high-quality vanilla beans (Tahitian is my favorite because it's so floral). For the best prices, shop online and buy your beans in bulk. You can also buy vanilla bean paste, which is essentially a jar of vanilla bean seeds in a vanilla-flavored gel so you can skip the hassle of dealing with the pod. For more on vanilla, read the sidebar on page 119.

2

BREAKFAST OF CHAMPIONS

Breakfast is one of my favorite meals of the day, and I'm fortunate to live in a city that feels the same way. We love our brunch in Portland. Sometimes, though, we crave leisurely week-ends when we can lounge around in our pj's rather than wait in long lines. Whether you're brunching at home or at a friend's, here are some of my favorite recipes that are definitely worth waking up for.

Aric~A~Strata

WITH MUSHROOMS, TOMATOES, AND FRESH DILL

I couldn't help naming this dish after an ex-boyfriend who helped me put my first cart together. Like this strata, he could make something awesome out of practically nothing. Take some eggs, cream, and stale bread, plus any odds and ends of cheese and vegetables you have lying around, and turn them into cheesy, savory, oven-baked decadence. It's seriously rich—just a little 8-inch-square dish will feed a crowd. And it's even better if you assemble it the night before—perfect for when you know you'll be too tired or hungover to cook in the morning. **MAKES 6 SERVINGS**

ingredients

- 2 LARGE EGGS
- 3 LARGE EGG YOLKS
- 2½ CUPS HEAVY CREAM
- SALT
- FRESHLY GROUND BLACK PEPPER
- ½ TEASPOON PAPRIKA
- ¼ TEASPOON FRESHLY GRATED NUTMEG
- ¼ CUP CHOPPED FRESH DILL OR OTHER FRESH HERBS
- 1 TABLESPOON PLUS 1½ TEASPOONS EXTRA-VIRGIN OLIVE OIL
- 5 PORTOBELLO MUSHROOMS (ABOUT 1 POUND), STEMMED AND CUT INTO 1-INCH CUBES
- 2 GARLIC CLOVES, FINELY MINCED
- 1 TEASPOON CHOPPED FRESH THYME
- ¼ TO ½ LOAF (8 TO 9 OUNCES) DAY-OLD BRIOCHE OR SOURDOUGH BREAD, CUT INTO ½-INCH-THICK SLICES AND EACH TORN OR CUT INTO 3-INCH PIECES
- ½ CUP CRUMBLED GOAT CHEESE
- 1 PINT CHERRY TOMATOES, HALVED
- 2 CUPS SHREDDED SHARP CHEDDAR CHEESE

instructions

- **GENEROUSLY BUTTER** the bottom and sides of an 8-by-8-inch glass baking dish. In a medium mixing bowl, whisk together the eggs, egg yolks, cream, ½ teaspoon salt, ¼ teaspoon pepper, paprika, nutmeg, and dill.

- **PUT A LARGE SAUTÉ PAN** over medium-high heat. When hot, add the olive oil and heat until shimmering. Add the mushrooms, season with salt and pepper, and sauté until the mushrooms are tender and their juices have evaporated, 5 to 7 minutes. Add the garlic and thyme and sauté until fragrant, about 1 minute. Remove from the heat.

- **POUR ABOUT ½ CUP** of the egg mixture into the prepared baking dish. Cover the bottom of the baking dish with a layer of bread, pressing it into the mixture. Sprinkle with half of the goat cheese, then one-third of the sautéed mushrooms, one-third of the tomatoes, and ½ cup of the Cheddar cheese. Pour one-third of the egg mixture on top and press to help saturate all the ingredients. Repeat the layering, starting with another layer of bread, the remaining goat cheese, half of the mushrooms, half of the tomatoes, and ½ cup of the Cheddar cheese. Pour half of the remaining egg mixture over the top and press. Add a final layer of bread and the remaining egg mixture, pressing to saturate. Cover with the remaining vegetables and the remaining 1 cup Cheddar cheese. Season with freshly ground black pepper. Cover the strata tightly with plastic wrap and refrigerate overnight. This will give it an extra-luxurious texture. But if you're in a pinch and need to bake it right away, it will still be a delight. Just try to wait 30 minutes to give the bread a chance to soak up the moisture before baking.

continued

- **WHEN READY TO BAKE,** preheat the oven to 350°F. Place the dish on the middle rack of the oven (with a sheet pan below to catch the drips) and bake, uncovered, until puffed and the custard is set in the center, about 1 hour. (If it's getting too dark too soon, tent it with foil, making sure the foil doesn't touch the cheese.) Let cool for at least 30 minutes to allow the bread to reabsorb the juices. Cut into six pieces and serve.

VARIATION:

Sweet Strata

- **FOLLOW THE RECIPE ABOVE,** adding 1/2 to 3/4 cup sugar (depending on how sweet you want it to be), the grated zest of 1 tangerine or orange, and 2 teaspoons vanilla extract (or the seeds scraped from 1/2 vanilla bean) to the egg mixture. Of course leave out the herbs, pepper, paprika, cheese, and vegetables. Instead use 2 cups berries or sliced fruit (if using apples, sauté them in butter first). Sprinkle the top with sugar and bake as directed.

TIPS

- *Contrary to popular belief, the bread for a strata or bread pudding doesn't have to be cardboard dry. It can be, but it doesn't have to be, so don't sweat it if you need to buy fresh bread for this. Just let it dry out in a 250°F oven for a few minutes to eliminate some moisture so that it can soak up more of the custard.*

- *This is a really flexible recipe, so you might add a bit more vegetables or bread than I do, or you might use a slightly smaller or larger pan. If, in the process, you end up with extra custard, save it to make a little French toast or a Monte Cristo sandwich the next day.*

- *Feel free to stray from this recipe and use what you have available. The strata can be made with most types of firm cheese—Gruyère and fontina are awesome choices—and any veggies you have handy—just give them a quick sauté or roast first. Think sautéed spinach, caramelized onions, or chopped roasted veggies like fingerling potatoes. And, of course, it wouldn't be breakfast without pork, so add a handful of chopped prosciutto, speck, ham, or cooked bacon, if you have it.*

- *If you have any leftover strata, you can slice it and reheat it in a sauté pan over medium-low heat with a little olive oil. Just brown it on both sides until warmed through.*

ingredients

- 3½ CUPS UNBLEACHED ALL-PURPOSE FLOUR
- ½ CUP ALMOND FLOUR
- 3 TABLESPOONS PACKED DARK BROWN SUGAR
- 1 TABLESPOON PLUS 1 TEASPOON BAKING POWDER
- 1 TEASPOON BAKING SODA
- 1 TEASPOON SEA SALT
- 1 CUP (2 STICKS) COLD UNSALTED BUTTER, CUT INTO ½-INCH CUBES
- 1⅓ CUPS BUTTERMILK
- 1 TEASPOON PURE VANILLA EXTRACT
- HEAVY CREAM FOR BRUSHING
- 1 CUP THICK JAM, FOR FILLING BISCUITS
- GRANULATED SUGAR OR VANILLA SUGAR FOR SPRINKLING

TIPS

- *Technically almond flour is a little more finely ground than almond meal, but you can use both interchangeably in my recipes. Almond meal has the added benefit of being sold at Trader Joe's for about half the price of almond flour, which is found on the gluten-free or baking aisle at many supermarkets.*

- *Be sure to use a thick, fruit-loaded jam. Lighter-style jams and jellies will get too runny in the oven and melt all over the place.*

- *If you want your biscuits to rise to impressive heights, make sure your biscuit cutter is sharp (no overturned drinking glasses) and don't twist while cutting. Otherwise you'll end up essentially pinching the top and bottom layers together, and the biscuits will have a hard time rising.*

Jammin' on the One

(BISCUITS 'N' JAM)

There's no excuse for the leaden, greasy hockey pucks some coffee shops try to pass off as biscuits. The only secret to making great biscuits is to go easy on the mixing. Honestly, this is one case where it pays to be a slacker. I add almond flour because I love how the nutty flavor really complements the fruity jam filling, plus it helps the biscuits achieve their amazing light and tender texture. **MAKES 16 BISCUITS**

instructions

- **PREHEAT THE OVEN** to 400°F. Line two large baking sheets with parchment paper or Silpats.

- **IN THE BOWL OF A 9-CUP OR LARGER FOOD PROCESSOR,** combine the all-purpose flour, almond flour, brown sugar, baking powder, baking soda, and salt and pulse a few times. Add the butter and pulse until pieces no larger than peas are formed. While pulsing, drizzle the buttermilk and vanilla through the feed tube. Continue pulsing until the dough just comes together and starts to pull away from the sides of the bowl. (A Cuisinart makes *the* best biscuits, but if you don't have one, you can mix the dough by hand in a large mixing bowl, using a pastry blender to cut in the butter until it's no bigger than peas. Or use a stand mixer fitted with a paddle attachment and mix in the butter on *low* speed so the butter doesn't fly out of the bowl.)

- **TURN THE DOUGH OUT** onto a clean, dry, lightly floured surface and gather it into a ball. Shape the ball into a disk and roll out the dough into an 11-inch circle that's at least ½ to ¾ inch thick. Use a round 3-inch biscuit cutter to cut out the biscuits, dipping the cutter in flour before cutting out each biscuit. You should get about ten biscuits. Gently gather the scraps, reroll, and cut out as many biscuits as you can, about six more.

- **PLACE THE BISCUITS** about 2 inches apart on the prepared baking sheets, eight per pan. Use your thumb to press into the center of each biscuit, making a well deep and wide enough to hold the jam (about half-dollar size). Freeze until firm, about 10 minutes. (You can pack the firm biscuits into a zip-top bag and freeze for up to 6 months.) Lightly brush the tops with cream, avoiding the dent. Fill each indentation with 1 tablespoon of jam. Sprinkle the tops with sugar and bake until golden brown, 18 to 23 minutes. Serve warm.

ingredients

- 2/3 CUP UNBLEACHED ALL-PURPOSE FLOUR
- 2/3 CUP PLUS 2 TABLESPOONS GRANULATED SUGAR
- 1/4 TEASPOON SEA SALT
- 2 TABLESPOONS UNSALTED BUTTER, MELTED
- 3 LARGE EGGS
- 3 LARGE EGG YOLKS
- 3/4 CUP HEAVY CREAM
- 1/4 CUP FULL-FAT GREEK YOGURT
- GRATED ZEST OF 1 LEMON
- 1/2 VANILLA BEAN
- 1/2 CUP FINELY CHOPPED HAZELNUTS (SEE TIP)
- 1 POUND (ABOUT 2 1/2 CUPS) FRESH WHOLE CHERRIES, PITTED (SEE TIP)

crumble topping

- 1/4 CUP OLD-FASHIONED ROLLED OATS
- 1/4 CUP UNBLEACHED ALL-PURPOSE FLOUR
- 3 TABLESPOONS PACKED DARK BROWN SUGAR
- 1/4 TEASPOON GROUND CINNAMON
- 1/8 TEASPOON SEA SALT
- 2 TABLESPOONS UNSALTED BUTTER, MELTED

BING CHERRY

Breakfast Clafoutis

A clafouti is a rustic, country French dessert, but its fruit-studded eggy base has always said "breakfast" to me. Honestly, a stack of flapjacks with maple syrup is sweeter, so I say it's time to make clafouti a legitimate breakfast option. To that end, I created this version with a fat dollop of thick Greek yogurt and a crumbly, buttery topping of sugar-spiced oats. If you're feeling a bit fancy, bake it in individual rame-kins. Or make it easy on yourself and use a large baking dish. **MAKES 6 SERVINGS**

instructions

- **PREHEAT THE OVEN** to 350°F.
- **IN A LARGE MIXING BOWL,** whisk together the flour, sugar, and salt. Whisk in the melted butter, eggs, egg yolks, cream, yogurt, lemon zest, seeds scraped from the piece of vanilla bean, and 1/4 cup of the chopped hazelnuts. Let the batter rest for 30 minutes.
- **BUTTER SIX 4-OUNCE RAMEKINS** or a 6-cup baking dish, coat with sugar, and tap out the excess. Arrange the cherries in the bottom of the dish(es). Pour the batter over the cherries and bake for 20 minutes.
- **TO MAKE THE TOPPING:** In a small mixing bowl, combine the oats, flour, brown sugar, cinnamon, and salt. Drizzle in the butter and stir until evenly moistened.
- **SPRINKLE THE CLAFOUTIS** evenly with the crumble, rotate the dishes from front to back, and continue baking until puffed, golden brown, and set in the center, 15 to 20 minutes more. Serve warm, sprinkled with the remaining 1/4 cup chopped hazelnuts.

TIPS
- *To toast the hazelnuts, preheat the oven to 350°F, spread the nuts in a single layer on a rimmed baking sheet, and toast until fragrant and beginning to color, 8 to 10 minutes. Cool and finely chop.*
- *Fresh, ripe, just-picked juicy cherries are the ultimate choice for this dish. If you have a farmers' market close by, march your butt down there. Bings are perfect, but a combination of Bing and Rainier would be wonderful, too. Taste the fruit and make sure it's sweet and flavorful, not watery. When fresh cherries are out of season, you can use fresh berries, sautéed apples or pears, or good-quality, organic frozen fruit.*

Thugs-'n'-Harmony

ingredients

- 2¹/₄ CUPS CAKE FLOUR
- ¹/₃ CUP SUGAR, PLUS MORE FOR SPRINKLING
- 1 TABLESPOON BAKING POWDER
- GRATED ZEST OF 2 LARGE LEMONS
- ³/₄ CUP (1¹/₂ STICKS) UNSALTED BUTTER, CUT INTO ¹/₂-INCH CUBES AND FROZEN
- ¹/₂ TO ³/₄ CUP COLD HEAVY CREAM, PLUS EXTRA FOR BRUSHING
- 1 TEASPOON PURE VANILLA EXTRACT

TIP
- *Zesting the lemon over the bowl is utilizing the entire lemon without losing lemony goodness—a good trick to know.*

I can never get enough lemon, so I always eat these light lemony cakes with gobs of lemon curd, but any kind of jam would be delicious. The rosy-hued Rhubarb Jam (page 137) pictured here is a particularly lip-smacking addition. You can even stash a bag of unbaked scones in the freezer for those nonfunctional mornings when measuring ingredients or adding to the pile of dishes in the sink is a frightening prospect. Serve with jam and butter or, my personal favorite, Luscious Lemon Curd (page 135). **MAKES 8 SCONES**

instructions

- **LINE A LARGE BAKING SHEET** with parchment paper. In the bowl of a food processor, combine the flour, sugar, and baking powder and pulse a few times. Add the lemon zest and butter and pulse until the mixture is pale yellow and the consistency of cornmeal. (If you don't have a food processor, just whisk the dry ingredients together in a large bowl, then cut in the zest and butter with a pastry blender.)

- **TRANSFER THE MIXTURE** to a wide mixing bowl. Make a well in the center and pour in ¹/₂ cup of the cream and the vanilla. Using your hand, draw the dry ingredients into the wet, mixing until just combined (you don't want to overmix, or the scones will be tough). If the mixture feels too dry and crumbly, add the remaining ¹/₄ cup cream.

- **ON A LIGHTLY FLOURED SURFACE,** form the dough into a patty about 9 inches wide and ³/₄ inch thick. Cut into eight wedges. Transfer each wedge to the prepared baking sheet and chill in the freezer for at least 15 minutes. (This will firm up the butter so it will create flaky layers when baked.)

- **PREHEAT THE OVEN** to 375°F. Remove the scones from the freezer, brush the tops with heavy cream, and sprinkle with sugar. Place on the middle rack of the oven and bake, rotating the pan from front to back halfway through, until the scones are golden brown and the tops are firm to the touch, 15 to 20 minutes. Cool for 10 minutes before serving . . . that is, if you can wait that long.

continued

- **MAKE AN IMPRESSION, LITERALLY, WITH YOUR THUMB** (move it around to make the indent half-dollar size), then fill with lemon curd or jam before baking. This is particularly cute if you cut the scones like biscuits instead of wedges. Or try making cherry, chocolate, and orange scones: In a small saucepan, heat 1 cup dried cherries with a liqueur such as kirsch or even simple syrup or juice. When the cherries are plump and moist, drain off the juices and fold the cherries into the dough along with orange zest instead of lemon zest and about 3 tablespoons chopped cacao nibs.

TIPS

- *Don't settle for bargain butter for this recipe. European-style butters, such as Plugrá, or my local fave, Crèmerie Classique, have a higher butterfat content that really makes a difference in texture and flavor.*
- *If you don't want to bake all the scones at once, freeze them until hard and pack them into freezer bags. Brush the frozen scones with cream, sprinkle with sugar, and bake at the same oven temperature but give them a few minutes longer: 20 to 25 minutes.*

ingredients

- 1/2 CUP PLUS 2 TABLESPOONS CHOPPED BITTERSWEET CHOCOLATE (ABOUT 3 OUNCES)
- 2 LARGE VERY RIPE BANANAS, PURÉED
- 1 1/2 CUPS UNBLEACHED ALL-PURPOSE FLOUR
- 1/4 CUP DUTCH-PROCESS COCOA POWDER
- 1 1/2 TEASPOONS BAKING POWDER
- 1/2 TEASPOON SEA SALT
- 3/4 CUP (1 1/2 STICKS) UNSALTED BUTTER, AT ROOM TEMPERATURE
- 1 CUP PACKED DARK BROWN SUGAR
- 3 LARGE EGGS, AT ROOM TEMPERATURE
- 1 TEASPOON PURE VANILLA EXTRACT
- 1/4 CUP (1 OUNCE) CACAO NIBS
- GRANULATED SUGAR FOR SPRINKLING
- FLEUR DE SEL FOR SPRINKLING

TIP

- *This also can be made as a lovely dessert. This amount of batter is perfect for a 4-cup mini-Bundt pan. Generously butter the pan. Baking times will vary, so check after 30 minutes; the top should spring back when touched and a knife inserted into the center should come out clean.*

Chocolate-Bananagasm
MUFFINS

The world doesn't need another blueberry muffin. And don't get me started on bran. But a chocolate muffin moistened with banana purée and sprinkled with sea salt? Hell, yes! These are so moist and tender yet not too sweet, and the cacao nibs add texture and a deeper chocolate flavor. When you have a couple of death-row bananas on your hands, skip the same old banana bread and whip up a batch of these. I adapted the recipe from a great food blog called "80 Breakfasts." Serve with salted butter or your favorite nut butter, such as fresh almond or peanut.

MAKES 12 MUFFINS

instructions

- **PREHEAT THE OVEN** to 325°F. Line 12 muffin cups with paper liners. Put the chopped chocolate in a medium metal bowl and put the bowl over a pan of barely simmering water. Heat, stirring, until the chocolate is just melted. Remove the bowl from the heat and let cool. Stir in the banana purée.

- **SIFT TOGETHER THE FLOUR,** cocoa powder, baking powder, and salt into a small bowl.

- **IN THE BOWL OF A STAND MIXER** fitted with a paddle attachment, cream the butter and brown sugar on medium-high speed until light and fluffy, 2 to 3 minutes. Scrape down the sides of the bowl. Add the eggs, one at a time, beating well after each addition. Beat in the vanilla. Scrape down the sides of the bowl. With the mixer on low, add the dry ingredients, cacao nibs, and chocolate-banana mixture and beat just until combined.

- **DIVIDE THE BATTER** equally among the prepared muffin cups. Sprinkle the tops lightly with granulated sugar and fleur de sel and bake for 15 minutes. Rotate the pan from front to back and bake for another 5 to 10 minutes. The tops should look crackled and slightly wet between the cracks. Let cool a bit before serving warm.

ingredients

cake

- 1 CUP UNBLEACHED ALL-PURPOSE FLOUR
- 3/4 TEASPOON BAKING POWDER
- 1/4 TEASPOON SEA SALT
- 1 TABLESPOON SOUR CREAM
- 1/4 CUP UNSWEETENED PASSION FRUIT PURÉE
- 3/4 CUP (1 1/2 STICKS) UNSALTED BUTTER, AT ROOM TEMPERATURE
- 3/4 CUP SUGAR
- GRATED ZEST OF 1 LEMON
- 3 LARGE EGGS, AT ROOM TEMPERATURE
- 1 TEASPOON PURE VANILLA EXTRACT OR SEEDS SCRAPED FROM 1/2 VANILLA BEAN (POD RESERVED FOR THE GLAZE)

passion fruit glaze

- 1/2 CUP UNSWEETENED PASSION FRUIT PURÉE
- 1/2 CUP PLUS 1 TABLESPOON SUGAR
- 1/2 VANILLA BEAN POD

- 16 OUNCES PLAIN, WHOLE-MILK GREEK YOGURT
- 2 PINTS FRESH BLUEBERRIES

TIP

- *Though it's freakishly delicious, with a bright tropical flavor unlike anything else, passion fruit purée, sadly and strangely enough, isn't a common item in most grocery stores. Look for it in the frozen section at Hispanic markets, where you might find it labeled maracuyá and sold by the Goya brand. You can also find it online at Amazon.com and PerfectPuree.com.*

"PASSIONS"
Breakfast Bundt Cake

While everyone else eats muffins for breakfast, I cut to the chase and serve cake. Because, really, except for the size, what's the difference? Actually this petite little Bundt is way more rich and buttery than most muffins could ever hope to be, but that doesn't mean it's not appropriate for the A.M. hours, especially when you serve it with dollops of thick Greek yogurt and a handful of fresh blueberries. The flavor is so bright, tangy, and passion-fruity, it's just the thing to wake up your taste buds.

MAKES 6 SERVINGS

instructions

- **PREHEAT THE OVEN** to 325°F. Butter and flour the bottom and sides of a 4-cup Bundt pan or 8-inch cake pan.

- **TO MAKE THE CAKE:** In a small bowl, whisk together the flour, baking powder, and salt. In another small bowl, mix the sour cream and passion fruit purée until blended.

- **IN THE BOWL OF A STAND MIXER** fitted with a paddle attachment, beat the butter, sugar, and lemon zest on high speed until light and fluffy, about 5 minutes. Scrape down the sides of the bowl. Add the eggs, one at a time, beating well after each addition. Beat in the vanilla. Scrape down the sides of the bowl. With the mixer on low, alternately add the dry ingredients and the passion fruit mixture, beginning with the dry ingredients and adding each in two increments.

- **POUR THE BATTER** into the prepared pan and smooth the top. Give the pan a couple of taps on the counter to knock out any large air bubbles. Bake on the middle rack until golden brown and the top springs back when lightly pressed, 35 to 45 minutes. Cool the cake in the pan on a wire rack for at least 20 minutes. Run a knife around the edge of the pan to loosen the sides of the cake, then invert it onto a plate.

- **TO MAKE THE GLAZE:** In a medium saucepan, combine the fruit purée, sugar, and vanilla bean pod and bring to a boil over medium-high heat.

- **REMOVE THE GLAZE** from the heat and brush liberally all over the cake. (You likely won't use all of it; save the little bit that's left to put in a smoothie or cocktail.) Serve with Greek yogurt and fresh blueberries.

streusel topping

- ¾ CUP UNBLEACHED ALL-PURPOSE FLOUR
- ¼ CUP OLD-FASHIONED ROLLED OATS
- ¼ CUP PLUS 2 TABLESPOONS PACKED DARK BROWN SUGAR
- ½ TEASPOON SEA SALT
- ¾ TEASPOON GROUND CINNAMON
- ½ TEASPOON GROUND CARDAMOM
- ¼ TEASPOON FRESHLY GRATED NUTMEG
- ¼ TEASPOON GROUND GINGER
- ½ TEASPOON PURE VANILLA EXTRACT
- 5 TABLESPOONS UNSALTED BUTTER, MELTED AND COOLED

fruit filling

- 2 PINTS FRESH MARIONBERRIES OR BLACKBERRIES
- ⅓ CUP GRANULATED SUGAR
- ¼ TEASPOON SEA SALT
- 1 TEASPOON GRATED LEMON ZEST

MARIONBERRY "CRACK"

Coffee Cake

Some things are so addictive you're willing to risk anything, even your political career, for just another taste. This isn't one of them—but it's close. The moist, fragrant cake, with its layer of lemon-spiked berries in the middle, is definitely something you'll want to trot out when friends come over for brunch; otherwise you're in danger of eating the whole thing yourself. The cinnamon-y, crumbly topping alone should come with a caution label. Consider yourself warned!

MAKES 12 SERVINGS

instructions

- **PREHEAT THE OVEN** to 325°F. Butter and flour a 9-by-13-inch baking dish, tapping out the excess.

- **TO MAKE THE STREUSEL TOPPING:** In a medium bowl, combine the flour, oats, brown sugar, salt, cinnamon, cardamom, nutmeg, and ginger. Stir until thoroughly combined. Mix the vanilla with the melted butter, pour into the dry ingredients, and stir until the mixture is evenly moistened and holds together when squeezed between your thumb and index finger.

- **TO MAKE THE FRUIT FILLING:** In a small mixing bowl, gently toss the berries with sugar, salt, and lemon zest.

- **TO MAKE THE CAKE:** Sift together the flour, salt, baking soda, baking powder, cinnamon, cardamom, ginger, and nutmeg into a medium bowl.

- **IN THE BOWL OF A STAND MIXER** fitted with a paddle attachment, beat the butter on medium speed until fluffy. With the mixer on medium-high, add the sugar and beat until light and fluffy, about 2 minutes. Beat in the vegetable oil, 1 tablespoon at a time, until incorporated. Add the eggs, one at a time, beating well after each addition. Scrape down the sides of the bowl. Add the sour cream and and vanilla and beat until incorporated. The mixture will be very light, smooth, and fluffy.

- **WITH THE MIXER ON LOW,** alternately add the flour mixture and buttermilk, beginning with the flour and adding each in two increments, and mixing after each addition just until incorporated. Remove the bowl from the mixer and fold in the toasted pecans with a spatula.

- **POUR HALF OF THE BATTER** into the prepared baking dish and spread evenly with a small offset spatula. Distribute the fruit filling evenly over the batter, leaving a ¼-inch border (so the fruit doesn't burn or stick to the pan). Top with the remaining batter and spread evenly. Sprinkle the streusel evenly over the top.

cake

- 3 CUPS UNBLEACHED ALL-PURPOSE FLOUR
- 3/4 CUP TOASTED PECAN HALVES (SEE TIP)
- 1 TEASPOON SEA SALT
- 1/2 TEASPOON BAKING SODA
- 1/2 TEASPOON BAKING POWDER
- 2 TEASPOONS GROUND CINNAMON
- 1 TEASPOON GROUND CARDAMOM
- 1/2 TEASPOON GROUND GINGER
- 1/4 TEASPOON FRESHLY GRATED NUTMEG
- 1 CUP (2 STICKS) UNSALTED BUTTER, AT ROOM TEMPERATURE
- 2 CUPS GRANULATED SUGAR
- 3 TABLESPOONS VEGETABLE OIL
- 3 LARGE EGGS, AT ROOM TEMPERATURE
- 1/4 CUP FULL-FAT SOUR CREAM
- 2 TEASPOONS PURE VANILLA EXTRACT
- 3/4 CUP BUTTERMILK

- **BAKE ON THE MIDDLE RACK** of the oven for 30 minutes. Rotate the baking dish from front to back and continue to bake until the top is a deep golden brown, springs back when lightly pressed, and a knife inserted in the center comes out clean, another 30 to 35 minutes.
- **LET COOL IN THE PAN** on a wire rack for about 20 minutes before cutting into squares and serving.

TIP

- *To toast the pecans, preheat the oven to 350°F, spread the nuts in a single layer on a rimmed baking sheet, and toast until fragrant and beginning to color, 5 to 8 minutes. Cool and finely chop.*

ingredients

- TWO 1/2-INCH-THICK SLICES BRIOCHE BREAD OR OTHER WHITE BREAD
- HIGH-QUALITY, FRUITY, EXTRA-VIRGIN OLIVE OIL FOR DRIZZLING
- 1 OUNCE CHOPPED BITTERSWEET CHOCOLATE, OR 2 TO 3 TABLE-SPOONS NUTELLA
- FLEUR DE SEL FOR SPRINKLING

Chocolate Panini

I hesitate to even provide a recipe for this crispy little morsel because it's so damn simple. It's like giving a recipe for cinnamon toast. You don't need me to tell you how to make that—I hope! Still, at the risk of being ridiculed, I offer up this recipe because it's something a lot of people have never thought to do. If you're one of them, make this and then thank me, because you'll find yourself grilling up a chocolate sandwich every time you get the munchies. Think of it as a poor man's *pain au chocolate*, with the added dimension of fruity olive oil and sea salt (which are musts, by the way, so don't skip 'em). It makes a tasty, speedy breakfast partner for your morning coffee. **MAKES 1 SERVING**

instructions

- **BRUSH ONE SIDE** of each bread slice liberally with olive oil. Arrange the chocolate (or spread the Nutella) evenly on the non-oiled side of one of the slices. Top with the other slice, oiled-side up. If you have a panini press, grill the sandwich until golden brown on both sides and the chocolate has melted, a minute or two.

  (If you don't have a panini press, heat a small sauté pan over medium-high heat. When hot, add 2 teaspoons of oil and the sandwich. Weight the sandwich with a heavy cast-iron skillet or a heat-safe plate topped with canned goods or a kettle full of water. [Go ahead and get creative; the goal is to flatten the sucker.] Cook until golden brown and the chocolate has begun to melt, about 1 minute. Turn and repeat on the other side, adding a little more oil if the pan seems dry.)

- **REMOVE THE SANDWICH** from the heat and let cool a minute. Then drizzle with more olive oil, sprinkle with fleur de sel, and cut crosswise into triangles.

TIP

- *I love the eggy decadence of brioche for this, so go hunt some down from your favorite bakery. If you have any left over, wrap it up well and freeze it for another use, like the strata on page 25. Any mild-tasting bread you have on hand will work, too. Challah is great, as are leftover slices from an artisan loaf, though the chocolate tends to melt through its larger holes.*

3

I DID IT ALL

FOR THE

COOKIE

I love old cookie recipes, with their deep histories and long traditions. Nostalgia, after all, is a big part of why I love to bake. Still, there's no reason why we can't take those old standbys and help them kick up their heels once in a while. I think our grandmothers would approve. In this chapter you'll find a few fan favorites, like shortbread and spice cookies, that get a lift in texture and flavor through the use of different flours and less-traditional ingredients. They're the new classics, with a thoroughly modern makeover.

Cooking WITH YOUR Senses

Turning batter into cake or dough into cookies is almost like alchemy. There are a whole host of things that have to happen at the molecular level for the transformation to occur. That's why successful baking requires precision, proper technique, and recipes.

And that's why so many people are scared to do it. But even within the confines of a baking recipe there is wiggle room—room for you to express your style, taste, and good sense. Follow a recipe like a robot, and you'll likely end up with cardboard results, but follow it while using all of your senses, and you'll make magic.

So relax. Engage. Put some good music on, pour yourself a glass of wine or tea, light some candles—do whatever it takes to get yourself "in the mood." Baking is a whole-body sensory experience.

It all starts with the ingredients you use. Get frisky with your fruit. Hold it, feel its weight in your hand. Look it over. Smell it. Ask for a taste. If it's not up to snuff, don't get it! Think about whether or not you can substitute a different fruit, or pick a different recipe. Let the quality of your ingredients guide you. There's no sense cooking with half-assed food.

Sometimes you need to educate your palate first before you can choose the right ingredient. Do a taste test: Try several kinds of chocolate, for example. Compare how they look, taste, smell, and feel on your tongue. Now you can make an experienced, educated choice and not be swayed by packaging. Train your palate, so you can trust it.

Whatever you're making, taste it at each stage, from the beginning to the end, so you're in tune with the recipe. You might find yourself inspired to add a different spice before you pop that cake in the oven, or maybe you'll want a different filling for that cookie.

And be sure to use the rest of your senses, too. Pay attention and watch as the cream whips. Does it look like it might be getting too stiff? Maybe it's time to stop. Smell the nuts toasting. Did you take them too far? Taste. Do you need to make a new batch? Listen to the lemon curd bubbling on the stove. Are the bubbles popping too fast? Maybe you need to turn the heat down so it doesn't burn. Touch the top of the cake. Does it feel springy, like cake should, or does it need more time?

Timing, temperature, the size or quality of ingredients—there are so many variables in baking that change from kitchen to kitchen and cook to cook. If you follow a recipe to the letter, without paying attention to your senses, you could end up burning, undercooking, or otherwise compromising the quality of the end product.

Be engaged from start to finish and trust yourself. Baking is a process that is technical as well as emotional; hence the term "taste the love." Always put THE LOVE in your food. This is one thing that you can't get from a box or buy from a store; it can only come from within.

- 1¼ CUPS UNBLEACHED ALL-PURPOSE FLOUR
- ⅓ CUP DUTCH-PROCESS COCOA POWDER
- ½ TEASPOON BAKING SODA
- ½ HEAPING TEASPOON FLEUR DE SEL, PLUS MORE FOR SPRINKLING (SEE TIP)
- ½ CUP PLUS 3 TABLESPOONS UNSALTED BUTTER, AT ROOM TEMPERATURE
- ⅔ CUP PACKED DARK BROWN SUGAR
- ¼ CUP GRANULATED SUGAR, PLUS ¼ CUP GRANULATED OR VANILLA SUGAR FOR COATING (OPTIONAL)
- 1 EGG YOLK, AT ROOM TEMPERATURE
- 1 TEASPOON PURE VANILLA EXTRACT
- ¾ CUP (ABOUT 4 OUNCES) FINELY CHOPPED BITTERSWEET CHOCOLATE
- ¼ CUP (1 OUNCE) CACAO NIBS

TIP

- *When using salt to sprinkle on top of a baked treat like this, be sure to use a flaky variety, such as fleur de sel or Maldon. Finely ground sea salt won't have the same impact, and coarse sea salt will be too much.*

Kir + Dorie ♡ ♡ Pierre

I love cookbook author Dorie Greenspan, and I especially love her recipe for World Peace Cookies, which she got from Parisian chocolate genius Pierre Hermé. They're intensely chocolate-y and buttery and salty, with an addictive melt-in-your-mouth texture. Although it's hard to improve on the original, I couldn't help tinkering with it a bit—but I think Dorie and Pierre would approve. **MAKES ABOUT 30 COOKIES**

instructions

- **SIFT TOGETHER THE FLOUR,** cocoa powder, baking soda, and salt into a medium bowl.

- **IN THE BOWL OF A STAND MIXER** fitted with a paddle attachment, beat the butter, brown sugar, and ¼ cup granulated sugar on medium-high speed until light and fluffy, about 2 minutes. Beat in the egg yolk and vanilla. Scrape down the sides of the bowl. With the mixer on low, add the sifted dry ingredients and beat just until combined. Stir in the chopped chocolate and nibs.

- **TURN THE DOUGH OUT** onto a sheet of waxed paper or plastic wrap. Form the dough into a loaf, cover with the waxed paper, and shape into a 12-inch log, pressing the sides against the work surface to flatten them, so the cookies will end up square. Refrigerate for several hours or until completely firm.

- **PREHEAT THE OVEN** to 350°F. Line two large baking sheets with parchment paper or Silpats. Put the remaining ¼ cup granulated sugar in a small bowl. Using a sharp knife, cut the log crosswise into ¼- to ½-inch-thick slices. (The dough is crumbly, so use a sharp knife and be patient. Thicker slices are easier to cut, but you don't want them too thick.) Roll each slice in the sugar until coated or just dip the sides. Place the cookies about 2 inches apart on the prepared sheets and sprinkle each with fleur de sel.

- **BAKE UNTIL THE EDGES ARE DONE,** the tops are slightly crackled, and the centers still look slightly underdone, about 12 minutes, rotating the sheets from front to back and between upper and lower racks halfway through.

- **LET COOL** on the baking sheets for a minute before transferring the cookies to a wire rack to cool completely. They will keep in an airtight container for at least 1 week.

- 1³/4 CUPS UNBLEACHED ALL-PURPOSE FLOUR
- 1/2 CUP HAZELNUT FLOUR (SEE TIP)
- 1 TEASPOON BAKING SODA
- 1 TEASPOON SEA SALT
- 1 CUP (2 STICKS) UNSALTED BUTTER, AT ROOM TEMPERATURE (SEE TIP)
- 3/4 CUP GRANULATED SUGAR
- 3/4 CUP PACKED DARK BROWN SUGAR
- 2 LARGE EGGS, AT ROOM TEMPERATURE
- 1 TEASPOON PURE VANILLA EXTRACT
- 1³/4 CUPS TO 2 CUPS (ABOUT 10 OUNCES) FINELY CHOPPED 70 PERCENT BITTERSWEET CHOCOLATE
- FLEUR DE SEL FOR SPRINKLING

TIPS

- *Hazelnut flour is finely ground hazelnuts. Bob's Red Mill and King Arthur Flour both sell it. But you can also make it yourself. Toast the hazelnuts in a preheated 350°F oven until fragrant and beginning to color, 8 to 10 minutes. Rub them between two kitchen towels to rub off as much of their dark, papery skins as you can. Let them cool before putting them in a food processor with 2 to 4 tablespoons unbleached all-purpose flour and pulsing until they are very finely chopped.*

- *To soften butter in a hurry, beat the crap out of it. Seriously. Just give it a couple of good whacks right in the wrapper. Get your aggression out. Peel off the wrapper, break off pieces by hand, and throw them in the mixer.*

Twisted Toll House

These cookies let you choose your own adventure. Hazelnut flour gives these classic chocolate chip cookies an incredible nutty flavor. But since it's oily, the more you use, the thinner the cookies get. Personally I love my cookies thin and crispy, as in this recipe, but if you prefer yours on the chubby side, follow the variation below. Either direction you go in, you can't go wrong. **MAKES ABOUT 24 COOKIES**

instructions

- **IN A MEDIUM BOWL,** whisk together the all-purpose flour, hazelnut flour, baking soda, and salt. In the bowl of a stand mixer fitted with a paddle attachment, cream the butter, granulated sugar, and brown sugar on high speed until light and fluffy, about 2 minutes. Add the eggs, one at a time, beating well after each addition. Beat in the vanilla. Scrape down the sides of the bowl. With the mixer on low, add the dry ingredients and beat just until combined. Stir in the chopped chocolate, using the larger amount if you're a chocolate fanatic. Chill the dough for at least several hours, or, if you can resist, overnight to give the flavors a chance to mature.

- **PREHEAT THE OVEN** to 350°F. Line two large baking sheets with parchment paper or Silpats. Drop the dough by 2-tablespoon portions (I use a 2-ounce ice-cream scoop) about 2 inches apart (they spread) onto the prepared baking sheets.

- **BAKE UNTIL GOLDEN BROWN,** 12 to 14 minutes, rotating the sheets from front to back and between upper and lower racks after about 10 minutes. Sprinkle the cookies with fleur de sel while still warm and let cool on the baking sheets for a minute before transferring them to a wire rack to cool completely. The cookies will keep in an airtight container for several days.

VARIATION:

Thick and Twisted Toll House

- **TO MAKE THE COOKIES** thicker and more like a classic Toll House cookie, increase the all-purpose flour to 2 cups, reduce the hazelnut flour to 1/4 cup, and add 3/4 cup chopped lightly toasted hazelnuts. Instead of finely chopped chocolate, use 1³/4 cups to 2 cups dark bittersweet chocolate chips.

ingredients

- 10 OUNCES BITTERSWEET CHOCOLATE, CHOPPED
- 3 OUNCES UNSWEETENED CHOCOLATE, CHOPPED
- 1/4 CUP (1/2 STICK) UNSALTED BUTTER, CUT INTO CHUNKS
- 3 LARGE EGGS, AT ROOM TEMPERATURE
- 1 CUP PLUS 2 TABLESPOONS SUGAR
- 1 TABLESPOON INSTANT ESPRESSO POWDER
- 2 TEASPOONS PURE VANILLA EXTRACT
- 1/4 CUP PLUS 2 TABLESPOONS UNBLEACHED ALL-PURPOSE FLOUR
- 3/4 TEASPOON BAKING POWDER
- 1/4 TEASPOON SEA SALT
- 1 1/2 CUPS BITTERSWEET CHOCOLATE CHIPS
- 1 CUP FINELY CHOPPED TOASTED PECANS (SEE TIP, PAGE 37)
- 1/2 RECIPE SEXY BITTERSWEET CHOCOLATE GANACHE (PAGE 132)

TIP

- *If you have a little leftover ganache, rejoice! You can melt it and drizzle it over ice cream or freeze it and use it later to make truffles or more cookies.*

TRIPLE THREAT
Chocolate Cookies

Chocolate cookies flecked with chocolate chips sandwiching a filling of chocolate ganache—these aren't called "triple threat" for nothing. Prepare to become addicted. The cookies are best when still soft after baking, so be careful not to overbake them. You might want to bake just one or two at first, to test how long it takes in your oven. These cookies do not freeze well. **MAKES 16 SANDWICH COOKIES**

instructions

- **PUT BOTH CHOPPED CHOCOLATES** and the butter in a medium metal bowl and put the bowl over a pan of barely simmering water. Heat, stirring, until the chocolate is just melted. Remove from the heat and let cool slightly.

- **IN A SMALL BOWL,** whisk together the eggs, sugar, espresso powder, and vanilla. Add to the chocolate mixture and whisk to combine. In another bowl, whisk together the flour, baking powder, and salt. Add the dry ingredients to the chocolate mixture and stir until evenly mixed. Stir in the chocolate chips and pecans. Cover the bowl with plastic wrap and chill until firm enough to scoop, several hours. If the dough ends up too firm to scoop, let it stand at room temperature for 5 to 10 minutes.

- **PREHEAT THE OVEN** to 350°F. Line two large baking sheets with parchment paper or Silpats. Drop the dough by 2-tablespoon portions (I use a 2-ounce ice-cream scoop) about 1 inch apart onto the prepared baking sheets. With your hand, flatten each portion into an even 1/2-inch-thick round. (Don't make them too flat, or they won't end up fudgy. Also, if the dough seems soft or sticky, lightly wet your fingers first to keep the dough from sticking.) Bake until the edges are cooked, the centers are soft but not wet, and you can feel a slight crust on top, 5 to 10 minutes, rotating the sheets from front to back and between upper and lower racks halfway through, (In my convection oven, they take just 5 minutes. They should be soft and fudgy, slightly underbaked but not raw. They will firm up as they cool.) Cool completely on the baking sheets on wire racks before removing the cookies with an offset spatula.

- **SPREAD THE FLAT SIDE OF HALF OF THE COOKIES** with 1/2 to 1 tablespoon slightly warm, soft ganache and top with the remaining cookies, pressing to help them stick. The filled cookies will keep in an airtight container in the fridge for up to two days, but be sure to serve them at room temperature for the best flavor.

Choosing Chocolate

There's no shortage of chocolate in the world, and that means there's a lot to consider when choosing one to cook with. First things first: Check out the percentage. The higher its percentage, the less sugar and the more chocolate liquor (i.e., the chocolate solids and cocoa butter derived from the cocoa bean) the chocolate contains. For example, a bar labeled 70 percent is made of 70 percent chocolate liquor and about 30 percent sugar. Unsweetened chocolate can be labeled 99 percent (with 1 percent made up of vanilla and lecithin). For most recipes in this book, you'll want a high-percentage bittersweet (a.k.a. dark) chocolate, something in the range of 64 percent to 74 percent.

Another thing to consider is how much cocoa butter the chocolate contains. Cocoa butter is fat, and fat helps you taste flavors better and offers a richer, smoother mouthfeel, so the more of it the better. The amount of cocoa butter in a bar isn't reflected in the percentage, and the amount varies from brand to brand, so check the labels. As long as there aren't any other additives like cream or cookies and as long as you're dealing with dark chocolate rather than milk chocolate, the fat content on the nutrition label will just reflect the amount of cocoa butter in the bar, and the higher the better.

Next you should consider how you plan to use the chocolate. If it's going into something with lots of other ingredients, you likely won't be able to taste the nuances of super-pricey premium chocolate, so go for something a step down that's still high quality.

Callebaut and Guittard are good workhorse brands, while Valrhona, Scharffen Berger, and Green & Black's are a little better and just as widely available.

When you're making something that's primarily chocolate, like truffles, go for the good stuff, maybe something made from a single-origin of bean, so you can really taste the fruity, nutty, or earthy notes the chocolate has to offer. There are many tiny top-notch producers in this category such as Felchlin in Switzerland, which I've discovered through shopping at Cacao in Portland. I love going to Cacao and geeking out with the shop's owners, Jesse and Aubrey. They're so good at helping me pick just the right varietal of chocolate for the dessert I have in mind. If you have a boutique chocolate shop in your neck of the woods, I highly recommend getting well acquainted with it.

Giddyup Cookies

ingredients

- 1½ CUPS UNBLEACHED ALL-PURPOSE FLOUR
- 1 TEASPOON BAKING SODA
- 1 TEASPOON GROUND SAIGON CINNAMON (SEE TIP)
- 1 TEASPOON SEA SALT
- 3 CUPS OLD-FASHIONED ROLLED OATS
- 1 CUP SWEETENED SHREDDED COCONUT (PREFERABLY ANGEL FLAKE)
- 1½ CUPS BITTERSWEET CHOCOLATE CHIPS
- ¾ CUP GOLDEN RAISINS
- 1 CUP (2 STICKS) UNSALTED BUTTER, AT ROOM TEMPERATURE
- 1 CUP GRANULATED SUGAR
- 1 CUP PACKED DARK BROWN SUGAR
- 2 LARGE EGGS, AT ROOM TEMPERATURE
- 1 TABLESPOON PURE VANILLA EXTRACT

With their crispy edges and chewy, oat-y middles, these babies bring out the cookie monster in me. They're one of the few things that make me thankful I'm a grown-up because it means I can eat as many as I want. Seriously, though, I can't decide what I like more: the cookies alone or sandwiching cream cheese ice cream (page 107) in the middle. They're killer both ways, especially hot out of the oven when the cinnamon is at its most fragrant. **MAKES ABOUT 30 COOKIES**

instructions

- **PREHEAT THE OVEN** to 350°F. Line two large baking sheets with parchment paper or Silpats.

- **IN A MEDIUM BOWL,** whisk together the flour, baking soda, cinnamon, and salt until well blended. Stir in the oats, coconut, chocolate chips, and raisins until well incorporated, breaking up any coconut clumps.

- **IN THE BOWL OF A STAND MIXER** fitted with a paddle attachment, cream the butter, granulated sugar, and brown sugar on high speed until light and fluffy, about 2 minutes. Add the eggs, one at a time, beating well after each addition. Beat in the vanilla. Scrape down the sides of the bowl. With the mixer on low, add the dry ingredients and beat just until combined.

- **DROP THE DOUGH** by 2-tablespoon portions (I use a 2-ounce ice-cream scoop), several inches apart (they spread), onto the prepared sheets and bake until puffed in the middle and golden brown, 15 to 18 minutes.

- **LET THE COOKIES COOL** on the baking sheets for a minute before transferring them to a wire rack to cool completely. They will keep in an airtight container for several days.

TIP

- *Saigon cinnamon, also known as Vietnamese cinnamon, has the best, most potent flavor. Thankfully, even supermarket brands like Spice Hunter and Spice Islands now sell Vietnamese cinnamon. Keep in mind that spices lose their potency over time, so just buy what you think you'll use up in six months to a year.*

ingredients

- 3³/₄ CUPS UNBLEACHED ALL-PURPOSE FLOUR
- 2 TEASPOONS BAKING SODA
- ½ TEASPOON SEA SALT
- 2 TEASPOONS GROUND SAIGON CINNAMON (SEE TIP, FACING PAGE)
- 2 TEASPOONS GROUND GINGER
- 1 TEASPOON FRESHLY GRATED NUTMEG
- ¼ TEASPOON GROUND CARDAMOM
- ⅛ TEASPOON GROUND CLOVES
- 1½ CUPS (3 STICKS) UNSALTED BUTTER, AT ROOM TEMPERATURE
- 2 CUPS GRANULATED SUGAR
- 2 LARGE EGGS, AT ROOM TEMPERATURE
- ½ CUP BLACKSTRAP MOLASSES
- 1 TEASPOON PURE VANILLA EXTRACT
- 1 HEAPING TABLESPOON PEELED AND FRESHLY GRATED GINGER (SEE TIPS)
- ½ CUP SUPERFINE SUGAR FOR COATING

OH SNAP!

Gingersnap Cookies

There's a veritable spice route in these cookies, not to mention a healthy glug of bold blackstrap molasses. It all adds up to some seriously kick-ass cookies. Eat them as is, or turn them into ice-cream sandwiches—try the Cream Soda Ice Cream (page 107). You can also crumble these babies up and mix them with oats for a crisp topping, use them instead of graham crackers in a cookie crust, sprinkle them on ice cream . . . You get the idea. They have a ton of uses, hold up great, and freeze well. **MAKES ABOUT 40 COOKIES**

instructions

- **IN A MEDIUM BOWL,** whisk together the flour, baking soda, salt, cinnamon, ground ginger, nutmeg, cardamom, and cloves until combined.

- **IN THE BOWL OF A STAND MIXER** fitted with a paddle attachment, beat the butter and granulated sugar on medium-high speed until light and fluffy, about 2 minutes. Add the eggs, one at a time, beating well after each addition. Add the molasses, vanilla, and grated ginger and beat until blended. Scrape down the sides of the bowl. With the mixer on low, add the dry ingredients and beat just until combined. Cover the bowl with plastic wrap and chill the dough for 1 hour or overnight if you can. (This dough benefits from resting overnight to develop its flavors.)

- **PREHEAT THE OVEN** to 350°F. Line two large baking sheets with parchment paper or Silpats. Put the superfine sugar in a small bowl.

- **SHAPE 2-TABLESPOON PORTIONS OF DOUGH** into balls, drop each into the bowl of sugar, and toss to coat. Place the balls 2 inches apart on the prepared sheets. Lightly press each to flatten slightly. Bake until the edges are set and the centers are puffy, 12 to 15 minutes. (Check after 12 minutes; don't overbake. After cooling, the edges will be crisp, and the middle will have a tinge of chewiness.)

- **LET THE COOKIES COOL** for a minute before transferring them to a wire rack to cool completely. They will keep in an airtight container for several days.

TIPS
- *Use a Microplane to grate fresh ginger. It quickly and easily cuts through the root's tough fibers like nothing else.*
- *Don't be tempted to use fresh ginger in place of dried, and vice versa. The flavors are completely different.*

Duke of Earl Cookies

ingredients

- 1½ CUPS UNBLEACHED ALL-PURPOSE FLOUR
- ½ CUP BROWN RICE FLOUR (SEE TIP)
- ½ TEASPOON SEA SALT
- 2 TABLESPOONS FINELY GROUND EARL GREY TEA LEAVES
- 1 CUP (2 STICKS) UNSALTED BUTTER, AT ROOM TEMPERATURE
- ½ CUP CONFECTIONERS' SUGAR, SIFTED
- 1 EGG YOLK
- 1 HEAPING TABLESPOON GRATED TANGERINE OR ORANGE ZEST
- ¼ CUP SUPERFINE SUGAR FOR ROLLING (SEE TIP)

Instead of tea and cookies, I like my tea *in* cookies. I usually reach for Earl Grey to bake with because it's earthy, citrusy, and perfume-y all at once, giving buttery baked goods like these delicate cookies a haunting depth. The tea also goes great with lemon and chocolate, so try tucking 1 tablespoon of (slightly firm) ganache between two cookies for a true tea sandwich, or dip the cookies in lemon curd.

MAKES ABOUT 40 COOKIES

instructions

- **SIFT TOGETHER THE ALL-PURPOSE FLOUR,** rice flour, and salt into a medium bowl. Add the tea leaves and whisk until blended.

- **IN THE BOWL OF A STAND MIXER** fitted with a paddle attachment, beat the butter and confectioners' sugar on high speed until blended but not fluffy, about 1 minute. Beat in the egg yolk and citrus zest. Scrape down the sides of the bowl and add dry ingredients. With the mixer on low, mix just until combined.

- **SCRAPE THE DOUGH OUT** onto a lightly floured surface and gather it into a ball. With floured hands, shape the ball into a 12-inch-long log. Wrap tightly in plastic wrap or waxed paper and twist the ends. Refrigerate until completely firm, about 1 hour.

- **PREHEAT THE OVEN** to 350°F. Line two large baking sheets with parchment paper or Silpats. Put the superfine sugar in a small bowl.

- **CUT THE LOG** crosswise into ½-inch-thick slices. Toss each slice in the sugar to coat. Place the cookies at least 1 inch apart on the prepared baking sheets. Bake until the edges are lightly golden and the cookies are firm, 15 to 20 minutes, rotating the pans from front to back and between upper and lower racks halfway through.

- **LET THE COOKIES COOL** for several minutes on the baking sheets before transferring them to a wire rack to cool completely. They will keep in an airtight container for at least 1 week.

TIPS

- *Just like regular rice flour, brown rice flour gives cookies a delicate crumb, but it has a nuttier flavor that goes really well with the tea. Look for it in the gluten-free section of the grocery store or at natural food stores. If you can't find brown rice flour, use regular rice flour.*

- *You can buy cartons of superfine sugar (C&H brand bakers' sugar) at many grocery stores, or make it yourself: Just whiz up some granulated sugar in your food processor until very fine. This is my go-to sugar for everything.*

TIPS

- *To turn these into delicious sandwich cookies, spoon 1 teaspoon of apricot preserves onto the bottom side of half the cookies. Top with the remaining cookies, bottom-side down, and sprinkle them with confectioners' sugar.*

- *Rice flour gives these cookies an incredibly tender texture. It's really worth seeking out, and with the explosion of gluten-free products on the market today, it's actually easy to find. Look for it at Trader Joe's, the gluten-free section at the supermarket, or online at Bobsredmill.com.*

CARDAMOM
Shortbread Cookies

These unbelievably tender, melt-in-your mouth cookies come at a price—they're very delicate, so handle with care. If an edge crumbles, just sprinkle on a little powdered sugar and deem them shabby chic. You can eat them alone, but to make them a little sturdier and even more pig-out worthy, I sandwich them with a dab of apricot preserves. Cardamom and apricots are BFFs, but so are cinnamon and strawberries, nutmeg and apple butter, and lavender and lemon, so don't be afraid to play with the recipe. Just remember a little spice goes a long way. **MAKES ABOUT 24 COOKIES**

instructions

- **SIFT TOGETHER THE ALL-PURPOSE FLOUR,** rice flour, cardamom, and salt into a medium bowl. Split the piece of vanilla bean lengthwise and scrape out the seeds with the back of a knife. Add to the bowl of a stand mixer fitted with a paddle attachment. Add the butter and confectioners' sugar and beat on medium-high speed until blended but not fluffy, about 1 minute. Scrape down the sides of the bowl and add the dry ingredients. With the mixer on low, mix just until combined.

- **SCRAPE THE DOUGH OUT** onto a lightly floured surface and gather it into a ball. Flatten the ball into a disk and wrap it in plastic wrap. Refrigerate until completely firm, about 1 hour.

- **PREHEAT THE OVEN** to 350°F. Line two large baking sheets with parchment paper or Silpats. Put the superfine sugar in a small bowl.

- **USING A SMALL ICE-CREAM SCOOP** or spoon, divide the dough into 2-tablespoon portions, and roll each portion into a ball. Slightly flatten the ball between your palms into a 1/2-inch-thick patty and toss it in the sugar to coat. Place the cookies at least 1 inch apart on the prepared baking sheets. Bake until the edges are lightly golden, 15 to 18 minutes, rotating the pans from front to back and between upper and lower racks halfway through.

- **LET THE COOKIES COOL** for several minutes on the baking sheets before transferring them to a wire rack to cool completely. They will keep in an airtight container for at least 1 week.

cranberry-port jam

- 1¹/₂ CUPS TAWNY PORT
- 1¹/₂ CUPS GRANULATED SUGAR
- 18 OUNCES FRESH OR FROZEN CRANBERRIES
- 1 TABLESPOON GRATED ORANGE ZEST
- ¹/₂ TEASPOON SEA SALT
- FRESHLY GROUND BLACK PEPPER
- ¹/₂ VANILLA BEAN

shortbread

- 4 CUPS UNBLEACHED ALL-PURPOSE FLOUR
- 2 TEASPOONS BAKING POWDER
- 1 TEASPOON SEA SALT
- 2 CUPS (4 STICKS) UNSALTED BUTTER, AT ROOM TEMPERATURE
- 2 CUPS GRANULATED SUGAR
- 4 LARGE EGG YOLKS
- ¹/₂ VANILLA BEAN
- ZEST FROM 1 LEMON
- CONFECTIONERS' SUGAR FOR DUSTING

DELLA'S AUSTRIAN
Shortbread Bars
WITH CRANBERRY-PORT JAM

These buttery bars with a ribbon of fruit in the middle are adapted from my awesome and forever-inspiring mentor, pastry chef Della Gossett. Her desserts were beautifully made, filled with whimsy, and insanely delicious. She's a true master craftswoman, and I'm indebted to her for teaching me how to become a thoughtful and creative baker and pastry chef. The cookies were part of her *mignardise* plate—essentially a little plate of tiny desserts served to guests *after* dessert, because, of course, one round of sweets is never enough. Since everything had to be just so, I had to cut these bars with laserlike precision, and we never served the chewier edges. I'm a corner person, myself, so getting to devour the toothsome little scraps made the whole cutting thing worthwhile. Plus, I often used them to bribe the hot line into giving me some braised lamb shanks—a fair trade in my opinion.

MAKES ABOUT 36 BARS

instructions

- **TO MAKE THE CRANBERRY-PORT JAM:** In a medium heavy-bottomed saucepan, combine the port, sugar, cranberries, orange zest, salt, and two or three good twists of black pepper. Split the piece of vanilla bean lengthwise, and scrape out the seeds with the back of a knife. Add to the pan along with the pod. Bring the mixture to a boil over medium-high heat, reduce to a simmer, and cook, stirring, until the berries burst and the mixture is deep burgundy and as thick as cranberry sauce, 15 to 20 minutes. Remove from the heat and let cool for a few minutes. Remove the vanilla bean pod and purée the mixture in a food processor or blender until smooth and easy to spread. Let cool, then transfer to an airtight container and refrigerate for several hours until cold. (The jam can be made ahead and will keep for several weeks in an airtight container.)

- **TO MAKE THE SHORTBREAD:** Whisk together the flour, baking powder, and salt.

- **IN THE BOWL OF A STAND MIXER** fitted with a paddle attachment, cream the butter and sugar on medium-high speed until light and fluffy, about 2 minutes. Add the egg yolks, one at a time, beating after each addition. Scrape down the sides of the bowl. Split the piece of vanilla bean lengthwise, scrape out the seeds with the back of a knife, and add the seeds to the mixing bowl. With the mixer on low, add the lemon zest and dry ingredients and mix just until combined. Divide the dough into two equal portions and shape each into a log. Wrap both in plastic wrap and freeze until very hard, at least 2 hours.

continued

- **PREHEAT THE OVEN** to 350°F. Butter the bottom and sides of a half-sheet pan (18 inches by 13 inches), then line the bottom with parchment paper. Use a box grater to quickly grate one log of the dough evenly over the sheet pan (do not press it in). Measure out 2 cups of the jam (save the remainder for another use, like topping biscuits or scones). Arrange dollops of jam evenly over the dough and spread to create an even layer, leaving a 1/4-inch border on all four sides. (You're not going for a thick layer of jam, but you shouldn't have bare patches either.) Grate the other log of dough evenly on top (again, don't press).

- **BAKE UNTIL THE TOP IS GOLDEN BROWN,** 40 to 50 minutes.

- **LET COOL** in the pan on a wire rack. When completely cool, cut into 3-inch-by-2-inch bars and dust with confectioners' sugar. The bars will keep in an airtight container for up to 1 week, or freeze for up to 6 months. (At the restaurant, we'd freeze them right in the pan and just cut what we needed. Just make sure to set them out 1 hour before serving, so they can come to room temperature.)

TIPS

- *The Cranberry-Port Jam is the easiest thing in the world to make and incredibly versatile. It goes great with everything from scones to a cheese plate. Heck, you can even serve it with your Thanksgiving turkey. But don't limit yourself to this jam when making the cookies. The Rhubarb Jam on page 137 is just as delicious, or you can try swapping the cranberries for cherries, adding sugar to taste.*

- *You can grate the dough using a food processor with a grating disk (cut the logs lengthwise into quarters first), but make sure the bowl is really big, so the grated dough doesn't get packed together. The shreds need to stay light and fluffy, so you can evenly distribute them.*

- *You don't have to cut these into bars. Use a biscuit cutter and cut them into fun shapes. Be sure to save the scraps to crumble over ice cream.*

- 1 CUP SALTED, ROASTED CASHEWS (SEE TIP)
- 1³/₄ CUPS GRAHAM CRACKER CRUMBS, FINELY GROUND (FROM ABOUT 10 TO 12 DOUBLE CRACKERS; SEE TIP)
- ¼ TEASPOON SEA SALT
- ½ CUP PLUS 2 TABLESPOONS UNSALTED BUTTER, MELTED
- 1 CUP BITTERSWEET CHOCOLATE CHIPS, SUCH AS GUITTARD EXTRA DARK
- 1½ CUPS SWEETENED SHREDDED COCONUT (PREFERABLY ANGEL FLAKE)
- 1 CUP CRUNCHED-UP POTATO CHIPS (PREFERABLY RUFFLES)
- ½ CUP BUTTERSCOTCH CHIPS
- ONE 14-OUNCE CAN SWEETENED CONDENSED MILK

Seven Layers of Sin Bars

Every Christmas, my mom would go into a baking frenzy, making at least fifteen different kinds of cookies. It was an all-out affair, and we packed them in tins and gave them to everyone. I still remember getting on the bus for school loaded down with tins for the bus driver and my teachers. "Here you go," I'd say sheepishly, feeling kind of shy and dorky. Looking back, I marvel at my mother's stamina and realize how very cool it was of her to channel her creativity and generosity into boxes packed with homemade treats that I'm sure everyone loved. These cookies were an especially big hit with me, and I almost hated giving them away. Now, of course, I love to share the sugar love, and I've made them even more sinful than the originals.

MAKES ABOUT 36 COOKIES

instructions

- **PREHEAT THE OVEN** to 350°F. Line a 9-by-13-inch baking sheet (called a quarter-sheet pan) with parchment paper. Butter the sides of the pan so that the edges of the cookies don't stick. Roughly chop the cashews and set aside.

- **IN A MEDIUM BOWL,** combine the graham cracker crumbs, salt, and butter and stir until the crumbs are evenly moistened. Press the mixture evenly onto the bottom of the prepared pan. Sprinkle the chocolate chips evenly over the crust. Top with the cashews, then the shredded coconut, the potato chip crumbs, and butterscotch chips. Drizzle the sweetened condensed milk evenly over the entire pan.

- **BAKE FOR 15 MINUTES.** Rotate the pan from front to back and bake until golden, another 10 to 15 minutes.

- **LET COOL** before cutting into 2-inch squares. They will keep in an airtight container for several days.

TIPS
- *You can buy roasted and salted cashews on the snack food aisle at the supermarket.*
- *You can use cinnamon graham crackers for extra kick, or even mix in some gingersnap crumbs. If you're in a pinch or feeling lazy, you can buy boxes of graham cracker crumbs at most supermarkets.*

- 2 CUPS UNBLEACHED ALL-PURPOSE FLOUR
- 1/4 CUP FINELY GROUND CORNMEAL (SEE TIP, PAGE 58)
- 1/2 TEASPOON SEA SALT
- 1 CUP (2 STICKS) UNSALTED BUTTER, AT ROOM TEMPERATURE
- 1/2 CUP PLUS 1 HEAPING TABLESPOON GRANULATED SUGAR
- 1 HEAPING TABLESPOON GRATED TANGERINE OR ORANGE ZEST (FROM ABOUT 1 1/2 TO 2 TANGERINES; SEE TIP, PAGE 58)
- 1 TABLESPOON PLUS 1 1/2 TEASPOONS FINELY CHOPPED FRESH ROSEMARY (SEE TIP, PAGE 58)
- 2 LARGE EGG YOLKS, AT ROOM TEMPERATURE
- 1/4 CUP SUPERFINE SUGAR FOR COATING

Rosemary's Baby

So. Damn. Good. That's what everyone says about these buttery little cuties. A dash of cornmeal gives them a nice crunch, and fresh rosemary and tangerine zest give them a one-two punch of herbal citrus flavor. They're perfect to nibble on with a mug of tea, or scoop yourself up a big bowl of lemon curd and start dipping. They're a little sturdier than my rice flour–laced shortbread cookies, so don't be afraid to pack them in a box and give them to a very lucky friend. **MAKES ABOUT 60 COOKIES**

instructions

- **IN A MEDIUM BOWL,** whisk together the flour, cornmeal, and salt.

- **IN THE BOWL OF A STAND MIXER** fitted with a paddle attachment, beat the butter and granulated sugar on medium-high speed until incorporated but not fluffy, about 1 minute. Scrape down the sides of the bowl. Add the citrus zest, rosemary, and egg yolks, one at a time, beating just until incorporated. Scrape down the sides of the bowl and add the dry ingredients. With the mixer on low, mix just until combined.

- **SCRAPE THE DOUGH OUT** onto a lightly floured surface, gather it into a ball, and divide the ball in half. With floured hands, shape each half into a 12-inch-long log, pressing the sides against the work surface to flatten them so that the cookies will end up square. Wrap tightly in plastic wrap or waxed paper and twist the ends. Refrigerate for several hours or until completely firm.

- **PREHEAT THE OVEN** to 350°F. Line two large baking sheets with parchment paper or Silpats. Put the superfine sugar in a small bowl.

- **CUT THE LOG CROSSWISE** into 1/3- to 1/2-inch-thick slices. Toss each slice in the sugar to coat. Place the cookies at least 1 inch apart on the prepared baking sheets. Bake until the edges are lightly golden, 15 to 17 minutes, rotating the sheets from front to back and between upper and lower racks halfway through.

- **LET THE COOKIES COOL** for several minutes on the baking sheets before transferring them to a wire rack to cool completely. They will keep in an airtight container for at least 1 week.

continued

Every Oven Is Different

Just because I say the cookies should bake for fifteen minutes doesn't mean that's how long they'll take in your oven. Everyone's oven is different. Sometimes there are hot spots or cold spots or the thermometer is off, or maybe the performance of your oven is just way better or way worse. The point is, don't just take my word for it or anyone else's. Only you can determine when your cookies are done. That's why I provide visual cues, too, so you'll know what to look for. So, as I've said before, cook with your senses: Turn on the oven light and watch the cookies' progress through the oven window (try not to open the oven door too much or you'll lose the heat), rotate the sheets if things are cooking unevenly, check the doneness early, and don't take them out until you've decided they're ready.

TIPS

- *Shopping for cornmeal can get pretty confusing. It comes in several grinds (fine, medium, and coarse) as well as several colors (white, yellow, and blue) and names (grits, polenta, etc.). I prefer finely ground cornmeal for pretty much all of my desserts—it has plenty of texture without being intrusive. Choose stone-ground cornmeal if you can, since it contains the germ, which makes it more nutritious. But the germ can also turn rancid, so store the cornmeal in the freezer, where it'll keep for up to two years.*

- *Whenever a recipe calls for orange zest, try to use tangerines or tangelos. They're much brighter in color and their flavor really pops.*

- *When using strong herbs like rosemary or lavender, use a light hand. You want a pleasing, subtle flavor, not something that overwhelms you like potpourri. You don't want your cookies to taste like soap.*

- 1½ CUPS (3 STICKS) UNSALTED BUTTER
- ½ VANILLA BEAN
- 1¼ CUPS TOASTED HAZELNUTS (SEE TIP, PAGE 29)
- 1 CUP PLUS 2 TABLESPOONS UNBLEACHED ALL-PURPOSE FLOUR
- 1¼ TEASPOONS SEA SALT
- 4 CUPS CONFECTIONERS' SUGAR, SIFTED
- 8 TO 9 LARGE EGG WHITES, AT ROOM TEMPERATURE
- ⅓ CUP (1½ OUNCES) ROUGHLY CHOPPED CACAO NIBS

vanilla syrup

- ¼ VANILLA BEAN
- ¼ CUP WATER
- ¼ CUP GRANULATED SUGAR

- BUCKWHEAT HONEY FOR DRIZZLING (OPTIONAL)

Hazelnibbies

The French have these awesome little almond teacakes, called *financiers*, that are soft and moist inside and almost candied on the edges. It's that sweet, light crunch as you bite into them that makes them so good. As I was coming up with my own version I couldn't help but turn to hazelnuts because they're such an iconic flavor here in the Pacific Northwest. Plus, they have more flavor than almonds, which means they can stand up to a few more nontraditional additions like cacao nibs and a drizzle of slightly bitter buckwheat honey. These make great ice-cream sandwiches with the Roasted-Banana Ice Cream on page 106. **MAKES 48 LITTLE CAKES**

instructions

- **PREHEAT THE OVEN** to 350° F. Butter the cups of a whoopie pie pan (the indentations should be 3 inches in diameter and 1 inch deep).

- **SPLIT THE PIECE OF VANILLA BEAN** lengthwise and scrape the seeds with the back of a knife. Add to a small sauté pan along with the pod and the butter and cook over medium heat until the butter darkens to a nutty brown and the solids drop to the bottom of the pan, 5 to 7 minutes. Remove from the heat and discard the vanilla bean pod (it won't be worth saving). Give the butter a good whisk to disperse the little browned bits and vanilla seeds into the liquid before pouring 1¼ cups of it into a measuring cup. (Those little bits have lots of flavor, so you want to include them.) If you have any extra butter, refrigerate it for another use.

- **IN THE BOWL OF A FOOD PROCESSOR,** combine the toasted hazelnuts and the flour and process until the hazelnuts are finely ground, like almond flour (see page 45). Transfer the mixture to a medium mixing bowl. Add the salt and confectioners' sugar to the bowl and whisk to combine. Add the egg whites and browned butter and whisk again until combined. Stir in the nibs.

- **FILL EACH OF THE INDENTATIONS** of the whoopie pie pan with 3 tablespoons of batter. Bake until golden, the sides look caramelized, and the tops spring back when lightly pressed, 18 to 20 minutes.

- **TO MAKE THE VANILLA SYRUP:** Split the piece of vanilla bean lengthwise and scrape the seeds with the back of a knife. Add to a saucepan along with the pod, the water, and sugar and bring to a boil over high heat, stirring occasionally. Let boil for 1 minute, then remove from the heat.

continued

- **BRUSH THE SYRUP** liberally over the still-warm Hazelnibbies. Serve warm, drizzled with buckwheat honey (if using). You can store any leftovers in an airtight container for several days.

TIPS

- *You can buy high-quality, Oregon-grown, roasted, salted hazelnuts from producers like Freddy Guys online. These Oregon nuts have the most incredible flavor and are well worth getting!*
- *Finely grinding nuts in a food processor is tricky because they want to turn into nut butter. The key is to pulse the nuts with flour. The oils are absorbed by the flour, which keeps the nuts from turning into a paste.*
- *You only need 1 cup plus 2 tablespoons (10 ounces) of browned butter, but because water in the butter evaporates during the process, you need to start with a little extra. It takes around 1½ cups (3 sticks) of solid butter to yield 10 ounces of browned butter.*
- *Traditionally financiers are made in a canoe-shaped mold, but I prefer using the shallow indentations of a whoopie pie pan, which you can find at cookware stores like Sur La Table. If you don't want to buy another piece of bakeware, you can substitute a muffin pan (add cupcake liners), but because the cups in a muffin pan are narrower, you'll end up making narrower Hazelnibbies. Use 3 to 4 tablespoons of batter per indentation. The baking time might vary, so keep an eye on them.*

4

LOVIN'
FROM THE
OVEN

I literally built my cart business on three cupcakes. That's about all I had on the menu when I opened, but people still came in droves. Why were mine so popular? They were incredibly tender and moist due to using oil instead of butter. Don't get me wrong. I love my butter, but sometimes it can leave cakes kind of dry. My other secret weapon? I brush my cakes after baking with flavorful simple syrups to help intensify the overall flavor of the cake and moisten it. If there's one thing I've learned from my years as a pastry chef, it's that people want an excuse to indulge in rich, decadent, crave-worthy desserts.

KRISTEN MURRAY'S
Rhubarb Meringue Pie

ingredients

pie crust

- 2 CUPS ALL-PURPOSE FLOUR
- 1 TEASPOON SALT
- 1 CUP (2 STICKS) VERY COLD UNSALTED BUTTER, CUT INTO 1/2-INCH CUBES
- 2 1/2 TABLESPOONS ICE WATER
- 1 TABLESPOON HEAVY CREAM

filling

- 4 CUPS CUT RHUBARB (PEEL ANY TOUGH SKIN AND SLICE INTO 1/2-INCH-WIDE PIECES)
- 6 LARGE EGG YOLKS (WHITES RESERVED FOR MERINGUE)
- 2 CUPS GRANULATED SUGAR
- 1/2 TEASPOON SALT

meringue

- 6 LARGE EGG WHITES
- 1/2 CUP GRANULATED SUGAR
- 6 TABLESPOONS CONFECTIONERS' SUGAR

My friend Kristen Murray, an amazing pastry chef in Portland who has worked in some of the top kitchens in the country, shared this delicious recipe, which has been in her family for generations. Rhubarb happens to be one of my most favorite things, and this pie, enriched with eggs and topped with fluffy meringue, achieves the perfect balance of sweet and tart. "It was my Great-Grandmother Nora's recipe," says Kristen. "When my grandmother passed, my mom and I brought home one of her favorite recipe boxes. Inside I found many treasured recipes for foods I loved eating, smelling, and helping to make as a child. This recipe was typed on blond card stock worn with time and use in Nana's kitchen. The word 'Mother' is in the right-hand corner, as Nana always liked to identify the person who gave her the recipe. I miss these beautiful Norwegian women, but making their recipes always makes me feel closer to them." **MAKES 8 TO 10 SERVINGS**

instructions

- **TO MAKE THE PIE CRUST:** In the bowl of a food processor, combine the flour and salt and pulse a few times. Add the butter and pulse until pea-sized pieces are formed. Sprinkle the ice water and cream over the mixture and pulse several times until the dough starts to come together. (To check, squeeze some of the dough between your thumb and index finger. It should hold together. Be careful not to overmix, or you will disrupt the delicate layers of butter and flour.) Turn the dough out onto a clean, dry work surface and gather it into a ball. Flatten the ball into a disk, wrap in plastic, and chill for at least 30 minutes.

- **REMOVE THE DOUGH** from the refrigerator and let it sit at room temperature for a few minutes to soften a bit. On a lightly floured surface using a lightly floured rolling pin, roll out the dough into a 12-inch round that's 1/4-inch thick. Make sure to turn the dough frequently as you roll to prevent sticking. (Use a bench scraper to dislodge any areas that stick to the work surface and dust the area lightly with flour.) Transfer the pie crust to a 9-by-2-inch pie plate and gently pat into place. Trim the edges, leaving a 1/2-inch overhang. Fold under and crimp. Freeze for 30 minutes.

- **TO MAKE THE FILLING:** Preheat the oven to 375°F. In a medium mixing bowl, combine the rhubarb, egg yolks, sugar, and salt. Pour the filling into the unbaked pie shell. Place the pie on the center rack of the oven and bake until the rhubarb is tender and cooked through, about 30 minutes. (The filling will look slightly jellied, like marmalade. To ensure the meringue doesn't begin to deflate, wait until the pie has finished baking before making it.)

- **TO MAKE THE MERINGUE:** In the bowl of a stand mixer fitted with a whisk attachment, beat the egg whites on medium speed until frothy, about 1 minute. With the mixer on medium-high, gradually beat in the granulated sugar, 1 tablespoon at a time. Continue beating until the whites hold medium-stiff peaks and look glossy. Remove the bowl from the mixer and sift the confectioners' sugar over the whites. Use a spatula to gently fold the sugar into the meringue (the confectioners' sugar enhances the texture). When the pie is ready, gently spoon the meringue on top and create decorative peaks using the back of the spoon.

- **PUT THE PIE BACK IN THE OVEN** and bake until the surface of the meringue is lightly browned, 8 to 12 minutes. Let cool before serving.

meringue shell

- 2 EXTRA-LARGE EGG WHITES, AT ROOM TEMPERATURE
- 1/4 TEASPOON CREAM OF TARTAR
- 1/2 CUP SUGAR
- 1/4 CUP FINELY CHOPPED TOASTED PECANS (SEE TIP, PAGE 37)

coffee mallow filling

- 1 1/2 CUPS MINI MARSHMALLOWS
- 3/4 CUP STRONG BREWED COFFEE
- 2 TEASPOONS UNSALTED BUTTER
- 1/8 TEASPOON SEA SALT
- 1 3/4 CUPS HEAVY CREAM
- 1/2 TEASPOON VANILLA EXTRACT
- 2 TABLESPOONS SUGAR

- 1/2 CUP SALTED CARAMEL SAUCE (PAGE 134), AT ROOM TEMPERATURE
- ONE 3- TO 4-OUNCE BAR OF HIGH-QUALITY MILK CHOCOLATE FOR GARNISH (MY MOM ALWAYS USED LINDT SWISS MILK CHOCOLATE)

MOM'S

Coffee Mallow Meringue Pie

The '70s weren't a complete faux pas. Here's another of my mom's treats that turns quirky ingredients into a fabulous dessert. It was my absolute favorite of my mom's desserts, and I asked for it every chance I got. The crisp meringue shell just melts in your mouth with toasty notes of pecans, and the coffee mallow filling balances the sweetness of the meringue. A drizzle of some salted caramel and a sprinkling of some grated milk chocolate deepen the flavors. **MAKES 8 SERVINGS**

instructions

- **TO MAKE THE MERINGUE SHELL:** Preheat the oven to 275°F. Generously butter a 9-by-1 1/2-inch glass pie plate.

- **USING A STAND MIXER** fitted with a whisk attachment or a hand mixer, beat the egg whites on medium speed until frothy. Add the cream of tartar, increase the speed to medium-high, and slowly beat in the sugar, 1 tablespoon at a time. Increase the speed to high and continue beating until the whites form medium-stiff peaks and look glossy. (The meringue should stay stiff and not droop when you lift the beaters, but if it looks dry or grainy instead of glossy, you've gone too far.)

- **GENTLY FOLD** the pecans into the whites. Spoon the mixture into the prepared pie plate. Using the back of the spoon, spread the meringue evenly over the bottom and up the walls of the dish.

- **BAKE UNTIL LIGHT GOLDEN BROWN,** about 45 minutes. Turn off the heat and leave the meringue shell in the oven with the door closed for another 45 minutes. The shell should have a nice golden color. Remove it from the oven and cool completely on a wire rack before filling.

- **TO MAKE THE COFFEE MALLOW FILLING:** Combine the marshmallows, coffee, butter, and salt in a medium saucepan and cook over medium heat, stirring occasionally, until the marshmallows have completely melted. Remove from the heat and let cool to room temperature.

continued

- **MEANWHILE,** using a stand mixer fitted with a whisk attachment or a handheld mixer, beat the cream, vanilla, and sugar on high speed until medium-stiff peaks form. Whisk a little of the whipped cream into the cooled coffee goo to lighten it and break up any lumps, then fold this mixture into the bowl of whipped cream until fully incorporated. Scrape the mixture into the cooled meringue shell, spread evenly, and smooth the top. Refrigerate for 1 to 3 hours before serving. (Don't assemble this pie too far in advance, because the filling will make the bottom of the pie shell slightly soggy. If you need to work ahead, make the shell and the cream up to 1 day ahead, but keep them separate.)

- **DRIZZLE THE TOP OF THE PIE** with caramel sauce and use a rasp-style grater to grate the chocolate over the top. Cut into slices and serve. (The edges of the meringue shell might crumble a bit when you cut it. Just dust with cocoa powder to hide the imperfections. Honestly, you're not going to care what it looks like because once it goes in your mouth you're going to be very happy.)

TIPS

- *Cream beats into nice fluffy clouds when everything is super-cold, including the bowl. Use a metal bowl and chill it in the refrigerator for 10 to 15 minutes before you begin. Make sure not to overbeat your cream, or it will break down and look curdled (because it basically turned into butter!).*

- *Don't let those yolks go to waste. If you don't have an immediate use for them, freeze them. When you've collected a couple more, you can defrost them overnight in the fridge and use them in something like Luscious Lemon Curd (page 135).*

- *Don't burn yer nuts! Burnt nuts have a bitter flavor that doesn't jive well with this or any other dessert. Keep a watchful eye and use your nose. When they've taken on a bit of color and smell nutty, they're done.*

tart dough

- 1¼ CUPS PLUS 2 TABLESPOONS UNBLEACHED ALL-PURPOSE FLOUR
- ⅛ TEASPOON SEA SALT
- ¼ CUP SUGAR
- ½ CUP (1 STICK) COLD UNSALTED BUTTER, CUT INTO ½-INCH CUBES
- 2 TO 3 TABLESPOONS COLD HEAVY CREAM
- 1 EGG YOLK

brown butter filling

- ½ VANILLA BEAN
- 4 TABLESPOONS UNSALTED BUTTER
- ¼ CUP PLUS 1 TABLESPOON SUGAR
- ¼ TEASPOON SEA SALT
- 1 LARGE EGG, AT ROOM TEMPERATURE
- ¼ CUP UNBLEACHED ALL-PURPOSE FLOUR
- 2 HEAPING TABLESPOONS CRÈME FRAÎCHE

- 1 PINT (ABOUT 2 CUPS) FRESH RASPBERRIES

Raspberry-Brown Butter-Crème Fraîche Tart

Notice how raspberry is the first word in the title? That's because this tart is all about the fruit. Yes, there's a rich tart dough made with egg yolk and cream. And yes, it's slathered with an amazing filling of vanilla browned butter and crème fraîche. But the filling is more of a flavorful base to support and contrast with all the bright fruit. Now, don't skimp and use extract instead of a vanilla bean when making the filling. You won't get the same depth of flavor as you do when you brown the seeds and pod along with the butter. You can, however, feel free to change up the fruit. You can use other berries, or even cherries that have been pitted—just cut them in half and toss with about two tablespoons of sugar. **MAKES 6 TO 8 SERVINGS**

instructions

- **TO MAKE THE TART DOUGH:** In the bowl of a food processor, combine the flour, salt, and sugar and pulse a few times. Add the butter and pulse until the mixture looks pale yellow and sandy.

- **IN A SMALL BOWL,** combine the cream and egg yolk. While pulsing, pour the mixture through the feed tube of the food processor. Continue pulsing until the dough forms a ball around the blade.

- **TURN THE DOUGH OUT** onto a lightly floured surface and gather it into a ball. Flatten the ball into a disk so it's not too thick and will be easier to roll out, wrap it in plastic, and chill until firm, at least 30 minutes.

- **REMOVE THE DOUGH** from the refrigerator and let stand at room temperature for a few minutes to soften a bit. Roll out the dough on a lightly floured surface using a lightly floured rolling pin, frequently turning it a quarter turn. (Use a bench scraper to dislodge any areas that stick to the work surface and dust the area lightly with flour.) Roll the dough out until it is ¼ inch thick and an inch or two longer than the length and width of a 4-by-13-inch removable-bottom tart pan. Carefully transfer the dough to the pan and gently press it into the pan, including the corners. Roll the rolling pin across the top of the tart pan to cut off the excess dough. Check around the top of the pan and make sure the dough is at least flush with the top, or make it a little higher. Prick the bottom of the tart all over and chill in the freezer until firm, 15 to 20 minutes.

continued

- **TO MAKE THE FILLING:** Split the piece of vanilla bean lengthwise and scrape out the seeds with the back of a knife. Add to a small sauté pan along with the pod and the butter. Cook over medium heat, whisking frequently, until the butter darkens to a nutty brown and the solids drop to the bottom of the pan, about 3 to 5 minutes. Remove from the heat and discard the vanilla bean pod. Measure out 3 tablespoons of the browned butter, making sure to get as much of the vanilla bean seeds and browned bits as you can. (You can save any extra butter for another use.)

- **IN A SMALL MIXING BOWL,** whisk together the sugar, salt, and egg until combined. Whisk in the flour, then whisk in the browned butter and crème fraîche until combined.

- **PREHEAT THE OVEN** to 400°F. Crumple a piece of parchment paper (to increase its flexibility so that it will conform more easily to the shape of the tart shell), then flatten it out and fit it into the chilled shell. Fill with pie weights, dried beans, or rice. Bake until the sides of the shell look set and golden, 10 to 15 minutes, then gently lift the parchment and beans and remove them from the tart. Reduce the heat to 350°F, and continue baking until the bottom is set and lightly golden, 5 to 10 minutes longer. (If the edges start to look too dark, cover them with strips of foil.) Let cool slightly on a wire rack for about 5 minutes before filling.

- **SPOON THE FILLING** into the prebaked tart shell, spreading it evenly over the bottom with a small offset spatula. Arrange the berries in an even layer on top. Bake on the center rack until the filling has puffed up around the fruit and is golden brown, about 25 minutes. (Again, if edges are getting too dark, cover with strips of foil.)

- **LET COOL** before cutting tart crosswise to serve.

TIPS

- *You can use any leftover scraps of tart dough to make mini jam tartlets. Roll it out and cut it into rounds. Drop a dollop of jam in the center of each round, and fold the dough over to make a turnover. Crimp the edges with a fork, chill until firm, and then bake until golden brown.*

- *Taste your fruit. If it's not very sweet, fold in 1 tablespoon melted apricot jam or seedless raspberry jam. Or use superfine sugar, which is absorbed more quickly.*

- *You can make the filling several days in advance. Let it come to room temperature before you use it, so it will be easier to spread.*

crostata dough

- 2 CUPS UNBLEACHED ALL-PURPOSE FLOUR
- 1 ROUNDED TABLESPOON GRANULATED SUGAR
- 1/2 TEASPOON SEA SALT
- 1/2 CUP (1 STICK) VERY COLD UNSALTED BUTTER, CUT INTO 1/2-INCH CUBES
- 2 TABLESPOONS VERY COLD RENDERED LEAF LARD, CUT INTO SMALL PIECES
- 1/4 CUP ICE WATER

caramelized apples

- 1/2 CUP (1 STICK) UNSALTED BUTTER, CUT INTO PIECES
- 1 CUP GRANULATED SUGAR
- 1/8 TEASPOON SEA SALT
- JUICE OF 1/2 LEMON (ABOUT 1 TABLESPOON)
- 1/2 VANILLA BEAN
- 3 MEDIUM-LARGE GRANNY SMITH APPLES (ABOUT 1 POUND, 9 OUNCES), PEELED, HALVED, AND CORED
- 1/4 CUP APRICOT PRESERVES
- HEAVY CREAM FOR BRUSHING
- SUPERFINE OR VANILLA SUGAR FOR SPRINKLING
- VANILLA BEAN ICE CREAM FOR SERVING

APPLE-APRICOT
Crostatas

I don't go in for frilly and fancy. I don't enjoy making seven-component architecturally complex desserts. But rustic sweets with depth of flavor? That's me in spades. And that's what these crostatas are all about. They're pretty but not pretentious, with a big hit of caramel-apple flavor brightened by the simple addition of apricot preserves. In the dough, I use a little leaf lard along with the butter. It makes the dough easy to work with, super-flaky, and adds a hint of savoriness that plays perfectly off the caramelized apples. If you've never added lard to your pie crusts before, consider this your call to arms. **MAKES 6 SERVINGS**

instructions

- **TO MAKE THE DOUGH:** In the bowl of a food processor, combine the flour, sugar, and salt and pulse a few times. Add the butter and lard and pulse until pea-size pieces are formed. While pulsing, slowly drizzle the ice water through the feed tube. Continue pulsing until the dough comes together. (The dough will start to ball up. If the dough seems dry, add 1 teaspoon more of cold water at a time, but don't get the dough too wet.) Turn the dough out onto a clean, dry, lightly floured work surface and gather it into a ball, kneading a few times. Flatten it into a disk, wrap in plastic, and chill for at least 30 minutes.

- **REMOVE THE DOUGH** from the refrigerator and let stand at room temperature for a few minutes to soften a bit. With a lightly floured rolling pin on a lightly floured surface, roll out the dough into a 15-inch circle that's 1/8 inch thick. Make sure to turn the dough frequently as you roll it to prevent sticking. (Use a bench scraper to dislodge any areas that stick to the work surface and dust the area lightly with flour.) If there is excess flour on your dough when you're done rolling, be sure to brush it off.

- **LINE A BAKING SHEET** with parchment paper or a Silpat. Use a 5-inch-diameter plate or biscuit cutter to cut out six 5-inch rounds and place them on the prepared sheet. (Try to cut them so that you don't have to reroll scraps to cut out more rounds.) Cover with plastic wrap and chill while you make the caramelized apples.

continued

- **TO MAKE THE CARAMELIZED APPLES:** In a 10-inch sauté pan that's at least 2 inches deep, stir the butter, granulated sugar, salt, and lemon juice. Split the piece of vanilla bean lengthwise and scrape out the seeds with the back of a knife. Add to the pan along with the pod and cook over medium heat, stirring occasionally, until the mixture is bubbly and turns a light nut brown, 5 to 8 minutes. Add the apple halves, cut-side down, and cook for 5 minutes, spooning the caramel over the apples to promote even cooking (lower the heat a bit if the caramel is getting too dark). Turn the apples over and continue cooking for another 5 minutes, spooning more caramel on top. (You want the apples to be cooked but still hold their shape and be slightly firm to the touch.) Remove from the heat and use a slotted spoon to transfer the caramelized apple halves to a clean plate. Let cool. (You can discard the leftover caramel in the pan, or use it to top the crostatas. Just add a little cream and whisk until smooth. Make sure to strain out the apple bits and vanilla bean pod.)

- **WHEN COOL ENOUGH TO HANDLE,** cut the apples into 1/2-inch-thick slices (four to six slices per half). Do not fan the slices or mix them up; keep them in the half-apple shape. They should be easy to cut yet slightly firm since they are going to bake for another 20 minutes—you don't want applesauce crostatas!

- **REMOVE THE CHILLED DOUGH** from the refrigerator. Drop 1 rounded teaspoon of apricot preserves in the center and spread it out a bit, leaving a 1-inch border. Place a caramelized apple half, cut-side down, on top. Fold the edges of the dough up against the apple, pressing the seams together where the dough over-laps. If the dough seems too firm to fold, let it stand at room temperature for a few minutes until slightly softened but no longer than 5 minutes, or it'll be too soft to work with. Freeze the crostatas until firm, about 30 minutes.

- **PREHEAT THE OVEN** to 400°F. Lightly brush the edges of the chilled crostatas with cream and generously sprinkle the dough and fruit with superfine sugar. Bake until golden brown, 20 to 25 minutes, rotating the baking sheet from front to back halfway through.

- **MELT THE REMAINING APRICOT PRESERVES** in a small bowl in the microwave for about 25 seconds, or in a small saucepan over low heat. (If it seems really thick, you can thin it out with a teaspoon of water if you want.) Let the crostatas cool slightly before brushing the tops of the apples with the melted preserves for added tartness and a pretty shine. Serve warm with the ice cream.

cupcakes

- 7 OUNCES BABY CARROTS
- 2 LARGE EGGS, AT ROOM TEMPERATURE
- $1/2$ CUP VEGETABLE OIL
- 1 CUP GRANULATED SUGAR
- SCANT $3/4$ CUP PACKED DARK BROWN SUGAR
- 1 TEASPOON VANILLA EXTRACT
- $1/4$ CUP BUTTERMILK, AT ROOM TEMPERATURE
- $1^1/2$ CUPS PLUS 1 TABLESPOON UNBLEACHED ALL-PURPOSE FLOUR
- $3/4$ TEASPOON BAKING POWDER
- $3/4$ TEASPOON GROUND SAIGON CINNAMON (SEE TIP, PAGE 48)
- $1/2$ TEASPOON SEA SALT
- $1/2$ TEASPOON SWEET CURRY POWDER
- $1/4$ TEASPOON BAKING SODA
- $1/4$ TEASPOON FRESHLY GRATED NUTMEG
- $1/4$ TEASPOON GROUND CARDAMOM
- $3/4$ CUP FINELY CHOPPED TOASTED PECANS (SEE TIP, PAGE 37)
- $1/2$ CUP GOLDEN RAISINS

curry syrup

- $1/3$ CUP WATER
- $1/3$ CUP GRANULATED SUGAR
- $1/8$ TEASPOON SEA SALT
- $1/4$ TEASPOON TO $1/2$ TEASPOON SWEET CURRY POWDER (DEPENDING ON HOW MUCH CURRY FLAVOR YOU WANT)

- 1 RECIPE CREAM CHEESE FROSTING (SEE TIP, PAGE 136)

Curried Carrot

CUPCAKES

Like Bert and Ernie or Batman and Robin, carrot cake with cream cheese frosting has to be one of the best duos in history. Still, even the most successful partnerships can use a little spicing up now and then. That's why I decided to enliven my super-moist carrot cake with a beguiling hint of sweet curry, which is composed of mostly sweet baking spices. (I get mine from The Spice House or Penzeys.) It's just a touch, so don't think that they will taste like tikka masala. **MAKES 12 CUPCAKES**

instructions

- **TO MAKE THE CUPCAKES:** Preheat the oven to 350°F. Line 12 muffin cups with paper liners.

- **PUT THE BABY CARROTS** in a medium saucepan and add enough water to cover. Bring to a boil and cook until very tender (they should be so tender you can easily mash them between your fingers), about 10 minutes. Drain. In the bowl of a food processor or blender, purée the carrots until completely smooth. You should have $2/3$ cup measured in a liquid measuring cup. Let cool for a few minutes.

- **IN A LARGE MIXING BOWL,** whisk together the eggs, vegetable oil, granulated sugar, brown sugar, and vanilla. Whisk in the buttermilk and carrot purée. In a separate bowl, sift together the flour, baking powder, cinnamon, salt, curry powder, baking soda, nutmeg, and cardamom. Stir the wet ingredients into the dry in two additions, mixing just until combined. Stir in the pecans and raisins.

- **DIVIDE THE BATTER** equally among the muffin cups. Bake on the center rack until the tops spring back when lightly pressed, 20 to 25 minutes, rotating the pans from front to back halfway through.

- **TO MAKE THE CURRY SYRUP:** In a small saucepan, combine the water, sugar, salt, and curry powder and bring to a boil over high heat. Continue to boil for 1 to 2 minutes to concentrate the mixture, bring out the curry flavor, and reduce any bitterness. (You can make the syrup a few days in advance; refrigerate until ready to use.)

- **WHILE THE CUPCAKES ARE STILL HOT,** brush the tops with the curry syrup. Let cool completely before frosting with Cream Cheese Frosting.

cupcakes

- 3 CUPS UNBLEACHED ALL-PURPOSE FLOUR
- 2³/4 CUPS GRANULATED SUGAR
- 1 CUP DUTCH-PROCESS COCOA POWDER
- 1 TABLESPOON PLUS 1¹/2 TEASPOONS BAKING SODA
- ¹/2 TEASPOON SEA SALT
- 1¹/2 CUPS BUTTERMILK
- 1¹/2 CUPS WARM STRONG BREWED COFFEE OR FRENCH-PRESSED COFFEE
- 3 LARGE EGGS, AT ROOM TEMPERATURE
- 1 TABLESPOON PURE VANILLA EXTRACT
- 1¹/3 CUPS VEGETABLE OIL

coffee syrup

- ¹/2 CUP STRONG BREWED COFFEE
- ¹/2 CUP GRANULATED SUGAR

- 1 RECIPE SEXY BITTERSWEET CHOCOLATE GANACHE (PAGE 132), WARM
- 1 RECIPE SALTED CARAMEL SAUCE (PAGE 134), AT ROOM TEMPERATURE

TIP

- *I've taken to impaling these cupcakes with shards of Ruffles potato chips as a garnish. The chips are quite dramatic, plus I love how they offer a counterpoint of salty crunch to the rich cupcakes.*

Highway to Heaven

CUPCAKES

Can you build your entire reputation on a single cupcake? Yes, you can. And I did. I put these foxy brown beauties on my menu the very first day, and they blew people's minds. They were like a gateway drug, luring people in with their coffee-chocolate-caramel decadence and opening the doors to my intense Ginger Island Cupcakes (page 79). Customers who had one came back a day later (sometimes just a few minutes later) to have more. Word spread, reporters came calling, and the rest is history. Now I couldn't take them off my menu even if I wanted to, which I don't.

MAKES 24 CUPCAKES

instructions

- **TO MAKE THE CUPCAKES:** Preheat the oven to 350°F. Line 24 muffin cups with paper liners.
- **SIFT TOGETHER THE FLOUR,** sugar, cocoa powder, baking soda, and salt into a large bowl. In a medium bowl, whisk together the buttermilk, coffee, eggs, vanilla, and vegetable oil. Add the wet ingredients to the dry ingredients and whisk just until incorporated and there are no lumps. (It's a thin batter, but it will bake up beautifully.)
- **DIVIDE THE BATTER** equally among the muffin cups, leaving about ¹/4 inch of room at the top. Bake until the tops spring back when lightly pressed, 20 to 25 minutes.
- **TO MAKE THE COFFEE SYRUP:** In a small saucepan, combine the coffee and sugar and bring to a boil over high heat. Continue to boil for 1 to 2 minutes to concentrate the mixture.
- **WHILE THE CUPCAKES ARE STILL HOT,** brush the tops with coffee syrup. (You'll use most but not all of it. Just discard the rest or use it in a cocktail.) Let the cupcakes cool completely before filling and frosting.
- **PLACE THE CARAMEL** in a squeeze bottle. Insert the tip into the top of each cupcake and squeeze in some caramel. (You'll see them plump up a bit, but don't fill them with so much that the cupcakes split.) Dip the tops in ganache, then tilt to shake off the excess. Let the chocolate set (it will be glossy but not runny) for about 30 minutes before drizzling with more salted caramel to serve.

- 1/2 TO 3/4 CUP SWEETENED SHREDDED COCONUT (PREFERABLY ANGEL FLAKE) FOR GARNISH

cupcakes

- 1 CUP CHOCOLATE STOUT BEER
- 1 CUP BLACKSTRAP MOLASSES
- 1/2 TEASPOON BAKING SODA
- 1/2 CUP GRANULATED SUGAR
- 1/2 CUP PACKED DARK BROWN SUGAR
- 3/4 CUP VEGETABLE OIL
- 2 HEAPING TABLESPOONS PEELED AND GRATED FRESH GINGER
- 1 1/2 TEASPOONS PURE VANILLA EXTRACT
- 3 LARGE EGGS, AT ROOM TEMPERATURE
- 1 3/4 CUPS WHOLE-WHEAT PASTRY FLOUR
- 1/4 CUP BUCKWHEAT FLOUR
- 2 TABLESPOONS GROUND GINGER
- 1 1/2 TEASPOONS BAKING POWDER
- 1 TEASPOON GROUND SAIGON CINNAMON (SEE TIP, PAGE 48)
- 1/2 TEASPOON KOSHER SALT
- 1/4 TEASPOON GROUND CLOVES
- 1/4 TEASPOON FRESHLY GRATED NUTMEG
- 1/4 TEASPOON GROUND CARDAMOM
- 1/8 TEASPOON YELLOW MUSTARD POWDER

ginger syrup

- 1/2 CUP GRANULATED SUGAR
- 1/2 CUP WATER
- 1 TEASPOON PEELED AND FRESHLY GRATED GINGER

frosting

- 1 RECIPE MAPLE CREAM CHEESE FROSTING (PAGE 136)

Ginger Island

CUPCAKES

Pastry chef Claudia Fleming created one of the moistest, gingeriest ginger-stout cakes on the planet in her cookbook *The Last Course*. I love that cake, but I couldn't leave well enough alone, so I started tweaking it to see how far I could take it. I added whole-wheat pastry flour and buckwheat flour for nutty heft, swapped out the Guinness for intense, locally made Rogue chocolate stout, and threw in more fresh ginger and a pinch of dry mustard for heat. The result is a seriously moist, seriously intense spice cake with a fluffy mound of maple cream cheese frosting and a sprinkle of toasted coconut. **MAKES 16 CUPCAKES**

instructions

- **PREHEAT THE OVEN** to 350°F. Spread the coconut in an even layer on a rimmed baking sheet and toast until golden brown, 3 to 5 minutes. Line 16 muffin cups with paper liners.

- **TO MAKE THE CUPCAKES:** In a medium heavy-bottomed pot, combine the stout and molasses and bring to a boil over medium-high heat. Turn off the heat and whisk in the baking soda. Set aside to cool and allow the foam to subside. When cool, whisk in the granulated sugar, brown sugar, vegetable oil, grated ginger, vanilla, and eggs (be sure the pot and the mixture are cool or the eggs might curdle).

- **IN A LARGE BOWL,** whisk together the whole-wheat pastry flour, buckwheat flour, ground ginger, baking powder, cinnamon, salt, cloves, nutmeg, cardamom, and mustard powder. Add the wet ingredients to the dry ingredients and whisk just until combined.

- **DIVIDE THE BATTER** equally among the muffin cups, leaving about 1/4 inch of room at the top. Bake until the tops spring back when lightly pressed, 20 to 25 minutes.

- **TO MAKE THE GINGER SYRUP:** In a small saucepan, combine the sugar, water, and grated ginger and bring to a boil over high heat. Continue to boil for 1 to 2 minutes to concentrate the flavors. (You can make the syrup a few days in advance; refrigerate until ready to use.)

- **WHILE THE CUPCAKES ARE STILL HOT,** brush the tops with ginger syrup. (You won't use it all. Just refrigerate the rest and use it in a cocktail or in the Fizzy Lifting Drink [page 123].)

- **LET COOL COMPLETELY** before frosting with Maple Cream Cheese Frosting. Place a large pinch of toasted coconut on the tops for garnish.

cake

- ³/4 CUP ALL-PURPOSE FLOUR
- 1 TEASPOON BAKING POWDER
- ³/4 TEASPOON SEA SALT
- TWO 7-OUNCE TUBES ALMOND PASTE (*NOT* MARZIPAN), BROKEN INTO PIECES
- 1 CUP PLUS 1 TABLESPOON GRANULATED SUGAR
- 2 LEMONS
- 2 TANGERINES OR ORANGES
- 1¹/2 CUPS (3 STICKS) UNSALTED BUTTER, AT ROOM TEMPERATURE AND CUT INTO CHUNKS
- 7 EGGS, AT ROOM TEMPERATURE
- ¹/2 TEASPOON VANILLA EXTRACT

citrus soak

- JUICE OF 1 LEMON
- JUICE OF 2 TANGERINES
- ¹/4 CUP GRANULATED SUGAR
- 1 TABLESPOON WATER
- ¹/4 VANILLA BEAN

- CONFECTIONERS' SUGAR FOR SPRINKLING
- 1 RECIPE LUSCIOUS LEMON CURD (PAGE 135) FOR SERVING
- 2 PINTS FRESH BERRIES, FIGS, OR CHERRIES FOR SERVING

TIP

- *I strongly urge you to spend a few bucks to get a Pullman loaf pan for this. Standard loaf pans scream "quick bread," and this cake deserves the more elegant form a Pullman loaf pan provides.*

Le Almond

This is my kind of hybrid. It's both a dense, moist almond cake and a bright, lemony teacake all at once—a perfect combination in my book. The cake is an awesome keeper; it stays moist for days, and the flavor seems to get even better!

MAKES 10 TO 12 SERVINGS

instructions

- **PREHEAT THE OVEN** to 325°F. Butter and flour a 13-by-4¹/2-by-2¹/2-inch Pullman-style loaf pan or two 9-by-5-inch loaf pans, tapping out the excess flour.

- **TO MAKE THE CAKE:** Sift together the flour, baking powder, and salt into a small bowl.

- **IN THE BOWL OF A STAND MIXER** fitted with a paddle attachment, beat the almond paste and sugar on low speed until the mixture is sandy and only small lumps remain, 3 to 5 minutes. Turn the mixer off and grate the lemons and tangerines directly over the bowl to catch all the oils. With the mixer on medium, gradually add the butter. Increase the speed to medium-high and mix until fluffy, 2 to 3 minutes. Scrape down the sides of the bowl. Scrape the paddle attachment to dislodge any clumps of zest and stir them back into the batter.

- **WITH THE MIXER ON MEDIUM,** add the eggs, one at a time, beating well after each addition. Beat in the vanilla. Scrape down the sides of the bowl and add the dry ingredients. With the mixer on low, mix just until combined. Use a spatula to give the batter a couple of folds to make sure everything is well incorporated. The batter will be very light and fluffy.

- **POUR THE BATTER** into the prepared pan(s) and smooth the tops. (If your Pullman pan comes with a lid, leave it off. If using loaf pans, divide the batter between the two.) Bake on the center oven rack until a knife inserted in the center comes out clean, 50 to 60 minutes. (The cake will take on a lovely, darkish red-brown color. Don't be afraid. It gives the cake terrific flavor and is such a pretty contrast to the lemon-yellow center of the cake.)

- **TO MAKE THE CITRUS SOAK:** Add the lemon juice, tangerine juice, sugar, and water to a medium saucepan. Split the piece of vanilla bean lengthwise and scrape out the seeds. Add to the pan along with the pod and bring to a boil over medium-high heat. Continue to boil for 1 minute to thicken and concentrate the flavors. Remove from the heat and remove the vanilla bean pod.

- **LET THE CAKE COOL** in the pan on a wire rack for about 20 minutes before inverting it onto a parchment-lined wire rack. Sprinkle with confectioners' sugar and brush liberally with the citrus glaze (discard any extra). Let cool completely before cutting into thick slices and serving with lemon curd and fresh berries.

Badonkadonk Shortcake

When a friend of mine had a birthday at the height of strawberry season, I knew shortcake was in order. But I also knew that setting a dinky little plate in front of her just wouldn't have the same ta-da! effect as a big layer cake. What to do? Make a honkin' shortcake, that's what. I cut it in half, filled it with saucy balsamic berries and crème fraîche whipped cream, and made a bright basil syrup to pass at the table.

MAKES 8 SERVINGS

ingredients

shortcake

- 2 CUPS ALL-PURPOSE FLOUR
- 1 TABLESPOON PLUS 1 TEASPOON BAKING POWDER
- 1/2 TEASPOON SEA SALT
- 1/2 TEASPOON CREAM OF TARTAR
- 3 TABLESPOONS PACKED DARK BROWN SUGAR
- 1/2 TEASPOON GROUND SAIGON CINNAMON
- 1/2 CUP (1 STICK) COLD, UNSALTED BUTTER CUT INTO 1/2-INCH CUBES
- 1 LARGE EGG
- 1/3 CUP HEAVY CREAM, PLUS MORE FOR BRUSHING
- SUPERFINE SUGAR OR VANILLA SUGAR FOR SPRINKLING

basil syrup

- 1 CUP TIGHTLY PACKED FRESH BASIL LEAVES
- 1/8 TEASPOON SEA SALT
- 2/3 CUP LIGHT CORN SYRUP
- JUICE OF 1/2 LEMON

strawberries

- 2 PINTS FRESH, RIPE STRAWBERRIES, HULLED AND HALVED (SAVE A WHOLE STRAWBERRY FOR TOPPING THE CAKE)
- 2 TO 3 TABLESPOONS GRANULATED SUGAR OR GOOD HONEY
- 1 TO 2 TABLESPOONS GOOD-QUALITY BALSAMIC VINEGAR

crème fraîche filling

- 1/2 CUP DIY CRÈME FRAÎCHE (PAGE 138)
- 1 CUP COLD HEAVY CREAM
- 1/4 CUP PACKED DARK BROWN SUGAR
- 1 TEASPOON PURE VANILLA EXTRACT
- CONFECTIONERS' SUGAR FOR DUSTING

instructions

- **TO MAKE THE SHORTCAKE:** Preheat the oven to 400°F. Line a baking sheet with parchment paper or Silpat. In the bowl of a food processor, combine the flour, baking powder, salt, cream of tartar, brown sugar, and cinnamon and pulse a few times. Add the butter and pulse until pea-size pieces are formed.

- **IN A SMALL BOWL,** stir the egg into the cream until thoroughly incorporated. While pulsing, drizzle the mixture through the feed tube of the food processor. Continue to pulse until the dough starts to form a ball around the blade. (The dough should hold together when squeezed between your thumb and index finger. If you need a tad more liquid, add an extra tablespoon of cream. But be careful: You can add more, but you can't it take away. Alternatively, you can mix the dough in a bowl by hand, cutting in the butter with a pastry blender, or mixing in the butter on low speed with a stand mixer.)

- **TURN THE DOUGH OUT** onto a lightly floured surface and knead it gently several times until it feels smooth and cohesive. Transfer the dough to the prepared baking sheet. With your hands or a rolling pin, form the dough into a 1/2-inch-thick, 8-inch disk. (Make sure the disk is at least 1/2 to 3/4 inch thick, or the dough will spread too thin while baking, making it difficult to cut in half once cooled.) Freeze for 15 to 20 minutes.

- **BRUSH THE TOP** with cream and sprinkle liberally with superfine sugar. Bake on the middle rack of the oven until puffed and golden brown, 20 to 25 minutes, rotating the sheet from front to back halfway through. Let cool completely before filling.

- **TO MAKE THE BASIL SYRUP:** In the bowl of a blender or food processor, combine the basil, salt, corn syrup, and lemon juice and purée until smooth. Strain the purée through a fine-mesh sieve and chill until ready to use.

- **TO PREPARE THE STRAWBERRIES:** In a medium mixing bowl, combine the strawberries, sugar, and balsamic vinegar and toss until evenly coated. Allow to macerate at room temperature for 15 to 20 minutes.

- **TO MAKE THE FILLING:** In the bowl of a stand mixer fitted with a whisk attachment, beat the crème fraîche, heavy cream, brown sugar, and vanilla until medium-stiff peaks form. Refrigerate until ready to use.

- **PLACE THE COOLED SHORTCAKE** on a level surface and use a serrated knife to gently cut the shortcake in half horizontally. (You can cut more evenly if you gently rotate the shortcake as you cut through it. Place your hand on top of the cake to help steady it as you go. Be careful, though, as the cake is fragile.)

- **CAREFULLY TRANSFER** the bottom half of the shortcake to a large, flat serving plate. Spoon the macerated strawberries and their juices evenly on top, leaving a 1/4-inch rim. Spoon all but 1/4 cup of the cold crème fraîche filling on top and spread it evenly over the berries. Carefully place the top half of the shortcake on top of the filling (don't worry if some of the edges crumble—this is a rustic dessert).

- **DUST THE TOP** with confectioners' sugar. Spoon the remaining 1/4 cup crème fraîche filling in one large dollop on top of the cake and plop the reserved strawberry into it. To serve, cut the cake into eight slices, wiping the knife clean with each cut. Serve with the basil syrup on the side. (This stuff is strong, so a little goes a long way.)

TIPS

- *If you have a tart pan with a removable bottom, you can use the thin metal bottom as a tool to transfer the shortcake layers without damaging them. The layers slide on and off easily.*

- *You can make the cake a few hours in advance and refrigerate it, but be sure to leave it out at room temperature for about 30 minutes before serving.*

- *If there's any basil syrup left, store it in an airtight container and use it for a cocktail, like a watermelon-basil margarita!*

- *If you don't want to make basil syrup, you can boil down the strawberry juices until they form a thick syrup that you can drizzle over the shortcake when serving. To make sure you have enough strawberry goodness in the middle of the cake, make a double batch of the strawberries, or spread 1/4 to 1/2 cup of strawberry preserves in the middle of the shortcake.*

- *If you have it on hand, you can swap out 1/4 cup of regular flour for almond flour to get an even more tender texture.*

Ultimate Brownie

These brownies are one of my most popular treats, and that's no surprise, considering they're mostly chocolate, butter, and sugar with just enough flour to hold them together. To make them extra fudgy, I use dark brown sugar and slightly underbake them, before I slather them with chocolate ganache. I like to serve them with fruity olive oil and a sprinkling of fleur de sel. Another can't-go-wrong choice? A drizzle of salted caramel, of course. No matter how you serve them, they are, in short, edible sin. **MAKES 14 BROWNIES**

ingredients

brownies

- 1⅓ CUPS UNBLEACHED ALL-PURPOSE FLOUR
- ¾ CUP DUTCH-PROCESS COCOA POWDER
- ½ TEASPOON SEA SALT
- 1 CUP (2 STICKS) UNSALTED BUTTER, AT ROOM TEMPERATURE
- 1½ CUPS GRANULATED SUGAR
- 1½ CUPS PACKED BROWN SUGAR
- 2 TABLESPOONS CRÈME FRAÎCHE OR SOUR CREAM
- 1 TEASPOON PURE VANILLA EXTRACT
- 4 LARGE EGGS, AT ROOM TEMPERATURE

coffee syrup

- ½ CUP FRENCH-PRESS OR STRONG BREWED COFFEE
- ½ CUP GRANULATED SUGAR

- ½ RECIPE SEXY BITTERSWEET CHOCOLATE GANACHE (PAGE 132)
- FRUITY OR GRASSY EXTRA-VIRGIN OLIVE OIL FOR DRIZZLING
- FLAKY SEA SALT, SUCH AS FLEUR DE SEL OR MALDON, FOR SPRINKLING

instructions

- **TO MAKE THE BROWNIES:** Line 14 muffin cups with paper liners. Preheat the oven to 350°F. Sift together the flour, cocoa powder, and salt into a medium bowl.

- **IN A STAND MIXER** fitted with a paddle attachment or in a medium bowl with a handheld mixer, beat the butter on medium-high speed until fluffy. Scrape down the sides of the bowl. Add the granulated sugar and brown sugar and beat on medium-high until the sugars are well incorporated and the mixture is light and fluffy, about 2 minutes. Beat in the crème fraîche and vanilla, then beat in the eggs, one at a time, beating well after each addition. Scrape down the sides of the bowl. With the mixer on low, add the sifted dry ingredients and beat just until combined. Use a spatula to give the batter a few good folds to make sure everything is incorporated.

- **DIVIDE THE BATTER** equally among the muffin cups. Bake on the middle rack until the edges are puffed and set and the center looks slightly undercooked (but not raw), 20 to 25 minutes.

- **TO MAKE THE COFFEE SYRUP:** In a small saucepan, combine the coffee and sugar and bring to a boil over high heat. Continue to boil for 1 to 2 minutes to concentrate the flavors.

- **WHILE THE BROWNIES ARE STILL HOT,** brush them with the coffee syrup. Cool on a wire rack for at least 20 minutes.

- **AS THEY COOL,** the brownies will fall a bit in the middle, which makes the perfect vessel for a dollop of the ganache (about 1 tablespoon). The brownies are at their best when they're still warm and the chocolate is ooey-gooey.

- **BEFORE SERVING:** Drizzle each brownie with extra-virgin olive oil and sprinkle with fleur de sel.

TIP

- *Whenever I have leftover cupcakes or brownies at the cart, I give them a second life as Chocolate-Chocolate Bread Pudding. I just break them up, put them in a baking dish, add some bittersweet chocolate chips, cover it all in the custard I use for the Sweet Strata (page 26), and bake until puffed and no longer wet in the middle. A garnish of Nutella Whoop (page 139) turns the dish into a true chocogasm.*

ingredients

corn bread

- BACON GREASE, LARD, OR BUTTER FOR GREASING THE PAN
- 1/4 VANILLA BEAN
- 8 TABLESPOONS (1 STICK) UNSALTED BUTTER
- 1/2 CUP BUTTERMILK
- 1 LARGE EGG
- 1 EGG YOLK
- 1/3 CUP FULL-FAT SOUR CREAM OR FULL-FAT GREEK YOGURT
- 1/4 CUP GRANULATED SUGAR
- 1/4 CUP BLACKSTRAP MOLASSES
- 1/2 CUP MEDIUM-FINE YELLOW CORNMEAL
- 3/4 CUP ALL-PURPOSE FLOUR
- 1 TABLESPOON PLUS 1 1/2 TEASPOONS BAKING POWDER
- 1 TEASPOON GROUND SAIGON CINNAMON (SEE TIP, PAGE 48)
- 1/4 TEASPOON GROUND GINGER
- 1/2 TEASPOON FRESHLY GRATED NUTMEG
- 1/2 TEASPOON SEA SALT

maple–white dog whoop

- 1 CUP COLD HEAVY CREAM
- 1/4 CUP GRADE B MAPLE SYRUP, PLUS MORE FOR DRIZZLING
- 2 TABLESPOONS PLUS 1 1/2 TEASPOONS WHITE DOG WHISKEY (OPTIONAL; SEE TIP, PAGE 88)
- CANDIED BACON CRUNCH (RECIPE FOLLOWS)

Corn Bread

WITH MAPLE–WHITE DOG WHOOP AND CANDIED BACON

For Southerners, corn bread is a starch. It's dry and savory, and great for sopping up all those dinner juices. But when you grow up on the sweet, tender muffins from the Jiffy box, like most other Northerners I know, it's no stretch to turn corn bread into dessert. I make a super-moist version with browned butter and baking spices, then top it with sweet, smoky, candied bacon and a dollop of whipped cream spiked with maple syrup and unaged "white dog" whiskey from House Spirits, one of Portland's best small-batch distillers. Now, don't go thinking moonshine and rotgut when you see the words "unaged whiskey." When properly distilled, unaged whiskey is smooth, with a creamy, sweet, cereal-like flavor that's not masked by the oaky vanilla notes you get from aging it in a barrel. It's definitely worth adding to your bar cart, but if you don't want to spend out, just swap it for a bourbon or whiskey you already have on hand, or omit the booze completely and add 1/4 teaspoon vanilla to round out the flavor. **MAKES 8 SERVINGS**

instructions

- **TO MAKE THE CORN BREAD:** Preheat the oven to 350°F. Coat the bottom and sides of an 8-inch cast-iron skillet or cake pan with bacon grease. Set aside. Split the piece of vanilla bean lengthwise and scrape out the seeds with the back of a knife and add to a small sauté pan. (Make sure the pan is shiny metal, not dark nonstick or cast iron, or you won't be able to see how dark the butter solids get.) Add the pod and 6 tablespoons of the butter and cook over medium heat until the solids drop to the bottom of the pan and turn a nutty brown, 3 to 5 minutes. Remove from the heat.

- **IN A MEDIUM MIXING BOWL,** whisk together the buttermilk, egg, egg yolk, sour cream, sugar, and molasses. In a large mixing bowl, whisk together the cornmeal, flour, baking powder, cinnamon, ginger, nutmeg, and salt. Stir the wet ingredients into the dry ingredients just until combined. Stir in the browned butter. Pour the batter into the prepared pan and bake until golden brown and the top springs back when pressed, 20 to 25 minutes. Remove from the oven and rub the top of the corn bread with the remaining butter.

continued

- **TO MAKE THE MAPLE–WHITE DOG WHOOP:** In the bowl of a stand mixer fitted with a whisk attachment or with a handheld mixer, whip the cream and maple syrup together on medium-high speed until soft peaks form. Whisk in the whiskey (if using), 1 tablespoon at a time. With the mixer on high, continue whipping until medium-stiff peaks form. (The cream can be made ahead and stored in an airtight container in the refrigerator for up to 2 days.)

- **PLACE A SLICE** of warm corn bread on a plate, top with a dollop of maple whipped cream, and garnish with the candied bacon and a drizzle of maple syrup.

VARIATION:

Praline Bacon Crunch

- **SPRINKLE** 2 to 3 tablespoons toasted, finely chopped pecans or hazelnuts onto the bacon before serving. To toast the chopped nuts, arrange them on a rimmed sheet pan and toast in a 350°F oven until fragrant and beginning to color, 5 to 8 minutes for pecans and 10 to 15 minutes for hazelnuts.

Candied Bacon Crunch

MAKES ABOUT $^3/_4$ CUP

- $^1/_4$ CUP GRADE B MAPLE SYRUP
- $^3/_4$ TEASPOON DIJON MUSTARD
- 2 GRINDS OF FRESH BLACK PEPPER
- 5 SLICES (ABOUT $^1/_3$ POUND) THICK-CUT APPLEWOOD-SMOKED BACON (SUCH AS NUESKE'S)

If the words "candied," "bacon," and "crunch" don't clue you in, let me warn you that this stuff is seriously addictive. You will not be able to stop nibbling it, so you might want to make extra. You don't have to save it for dessert, either. It would be perfect next to your eggs at breakfast if you don't chop it up.

- **PREHEAT THE OVEN** to 400°F. Line a rimmed baking sheet with parchment paper or a Silpat and place a metal oven-safe rack (like a cooling rack for cookies) on top.

- **IN A SMALL BOWL,** mix together the maple syrup, mustard, and pepper. Dip the bacon in the maple mixture, coating both sides liberally, and arrange on the rack in a single layer. Bake for 10 minutes. Flip the bacon over, baste with more maple mixture, and bake for another 10 minutes, basting once more during the last 5 minutes of baking. The bacon will take on a rich caramelized color and a lacquered sheen.

- **IF YOU WANT TO TEAR THE BACON** into pieces, let it cool completely first. Or you can cut each slice in half and serve.

Love Thy Lard

Lard is a wonderful thing. When chilled it doesn't get as hard as butter, so your pie crusts are more malleable and easier to work with.

It also takes longer to melt than butter, resulting in the flakiest piecrusts imaginable. On top of that, it has ever so slight hints of savoriness, which really bring out the sweet flavors of fruit. I love a lard crust with a fragrant apple pie, or just a little lard mixed into a butter crust, as in the Apple-Apricot Crostatas (page 72).

You've probably seen giant tubs of unrefrigerated lard at the supermarket, but, trust me, you don't want to use those. They're partially hydrogenated and not made with the highest-quality fat. For pie crusts, you want the best. That means leaf fat rendered with care. Leaf fat, which is the highest grade of pig fat, is obtained from around the kidneys and inside the loin. It's great for baking because it has very little pork flavor if you render it right. Don't confuse it with fatback, which comes from the pig's back and is a little harder. Fatback isn't bad; it's just more appropriate for frying than baking.

Some butcher shops (usually either high end or old school) will sell rendered lard (it should be refrigerated), but you might have an easier time finding unrendered. Besides, it's cheaper, often cheaper by the pound than butter. So don't be afraid to pick some up and render it yourself. Get at least a pound, as quarter pounds of fat will yield about 2 cups of rendered lard.

To offer you the best rendering instructions, I consulted Jason French at Ned Ludd, one of my favorite restaurants in Portland. Jason makes everything in a brick oven using the best local ingredients—including plenty of lard from local hogs—and his simple and beautifully rustic approach to cooking is right up my alley.

Jason and I can assure you that rendering lard is easy. But it's a slow process, so you have to plan ahead. First, be prepared for your house to smell very rich and savory and porky while you do this, so you might want to open a window. Chop the fat into ½-inch cubes or coarsely grind it, as Jason does. Put the fat in a deep, heavy-bottomed pot and add enough water to cover it. "The water basically acts as a barrier between the fat and the heating surface," says Jason. "It is important to do it slowly, so there is no browning of the fats or any solids. Browning limits the quality and affects the flavor." In other words, your lard will end up tasting meaty.

Bring the lard and water to a boil over medium heat, stirring occasionally. Reduce the heat to the lowest setting and continue to cook. "It will take several hours," says Jason. "By the time all the water has evaporated, the rendering process is almost complete." You should see the solids (a.k.a. cracklins) float to the surface. You can also slowly render the lard in a slow cooker set on low (it'll take all day), or in a 200°F oven.

Strain the fat through a cheesecloth-lined sieve into a mason jar and allow to cool (it'll solidify and look white). Cover and refrigerate or freeze. It'll keep for months.

Jason gets his fat (and pork) from Afton Field Farm and Square Peg Farm near Portland. If you're a local, you can stop into Laurelhurst Market for rendered leaf lard or Gartner's Country Meats for actual leaf fat. If you don't live in Portland, ask around at real butcher shops near you. If they don't carry leaf lard, they might be able to order it for you. Or shop for rendered leaf lard online.

Warm puddings, cool ice creams, luscious custards, and icy sorbets—there's something about spoonable desserts that strikes a deep chord in me and most other people, too. Is it the creamy, dreamy goodness? The way they're effortless to eat? It's likely both, and it all adds up to irresistible in my book. The desserts in this chapter are all built around versatile bases, from the Black Cow Panna Cotta to the Cherry Lambic Sorbet, which provide the perfect playground for adding fun additions like a reduced root beer drizzle or a tart lambic beer. It also means you can add your own creative impulses and pair them with the flavors and components you love best.

Vanilla Bean Risotto

WITH RUBY GRAPEFRUIT AND CARA CARA ORANGES

ingredients

fruit

- 1 RUBY RED GRAPEFRUIT (ABOUT 12 TO 13 OUNCES)
- 2 CARA CARA ORANGES (ABOUT 6 OUNCES EACH; SEE TIP, FACING PAGE)
- 1 TO 2 TABLESPOONS GRANULATED SUGAR OR GOOD HONEY

risotto

- 3 1/2 CUPS HALF-AND-HALF
- GRATED ZEST OF 1 CARA CARA ORANGE
- 1 VANILLA BEAN
- 2 TABLESPOONS (1/4 STICK) UNSALTED BUTTER
- 1 CUP ARBORIO RICE
- 1/2 CUP HEAVY CREAM, PLUS EXTRA AS NEEDED
- 1/8 TEASPOON SEA SALT
- 1/4 CUP PLUS 2 TABLESPOONS SUPERFINE SUGAR
- 2 TO 3 TABLESPOONS GRAND MARNIER (OPTIONAL BUT OH SO GOOD!)

Why limit risotto to the main course? It's rice. Rice is happy in desserts. It's time to free risotto from its chicken-stock bonds and let it frolic with sugar and spice and everything nice in a creamy, luscious last course. What's so wonderful about this recipe, aside from its delicious decadence, is that it really can be topped with just about anything. Citrus provides a bright, tart flavor contrast, but fresh or roasted figs, sautéed apples, summer berries, or fruit compote of any kind would also go really well with it. Even a dark chocolate sauce would be awesome with the risotto's citrus notes. **MAKES 4 TO 6 SERVINGS**

instructions

- **TO PREPARE THE FRUIT:** Use a sharp knife to slice the peel off the top and bottom of the grapefruit. Working on a flat surface, slice away the peel (including the white pith), following the curve of the fruit, on all sides. Working directly over a medium bowl to catch any juices and the segments as they are released, cut along the white membranes on both sides of each segment. With a Microplane, remove the zest from one of the oranges and set aside. Remove the segments of both oranges as you did with the grapefruit. (This technique is called supreming the citrus.) Sprinkle the segments with the granulated sugar and toss to combine. Allow to macerate at room temperature for 30 minutes.

- **TO MAKE THE RISOTTO:** In a medium saucepan combine the half-and-half and orange zest. Split the vanilla bean lengthwise and scrape out the seeds with the back of a knife. Add to the pan along with the pod and bring to a simmer over medium-high heat, stirring occasionally. Remove from the heat.

- **IN A LARGE SAUCEPAN,** melt the butter over medium heat. Add the rice and sauté until it begins to look translucent, 3 to 5 minutes. Add 1/2 cup of the half-and-half mixture and cook, stirring, until the liquid has been absorbed. Repeat this procedure until all the liquid has been absorbed and the rice is al dente (tender but not mushy, with just a hint of firmness in the middle), 25 minutes to 35 minutes. (Don't discard the vanilla bean pod. Rinse, let dry, and save for another use.)

- **REDUCE THE HEAT** to low and stir the cream, salt, and superfine sugar into the risotto. Continue stirring until the cream has been absorbed and the rice is fully tender, another 5 minutes. (Taste the risotto. If the rice still seems too firm, you can add a little more cream or half-and-half and cook it a little longer.) Remove from the heat and stir in the Grand Marnier (if using). Let stand for several minutes before serving.

- **GIVE THE RISOTTO** one more stir before dividing it among serving bowls. Use a slotted spoon to scoop up the macerated citrus fruit, leaving the juices behind, and distribute it among the bowls to serve. (If the risotto has become too thick before serving, stir in a tablespoon or two of cream to loosen it up. It should be loose and creamy, not soupy or pasty.)

TIPS

- *Refrigerate leftover risotto in an airtight container. Reheat with a little cream in the microwave or in a saucepan set over low heat.*
- *Cara Cara oranges are a type of navel orange that has rosy flesh. They are low in acid and slightly sweeter than a regular orange, with hints of rose and berry flavors. Peak season for cara cara oranges is late November through January. Look for them at specialty markets. If you can't find them, you can substitute tangerines.*
- *When cooking the risotto, make sure the heat is not too high, or you will burn the rice and the liquid will evaporate before the rice can absorb it. Moderate heat and constant stirring are what you need to produce rich, creamy risotto that's fully cooked.*

- 3 EGG YOLKS
- 1/3 CUP GRANULATED SUGAR, PLUS 3 TABLESPOONS
- 1/4 CUP MARSALA WINE, PLUS 3 TABLESPOONS
- 8 OUNCES MASCARPONE CHEESE
- 1/4 TEASPOON GROUND SAIGON CINNAMON (SEE TIP, PAGE 48)
- 1 CUP HEAVY CREAM
- 1 TEASPOON PURE VANILLA EXTRACT
- 1 1/4 CUPS STRONG BREWED COFFEE
- 1/4 CUP (ABOUT 2 SHOTS) ESPRESSO
- 8 TO 10 UNGLAZED OLD-FASHIONED DONUTS
- COCOA POWDER OR SHAVED CHOCOLATE FOR DUSTING

Donut~Misu
(COFFEE 'N' DONUTS)

Tiramisu is a delightful thing—except for the ladyfingers. I don't see the point of using anything that dry and tasteless in a dessert, even if it is soaked in espresso. If you're going to dunk something in coffee, it should be a donut, right? Between the donuts, coffee, and Marsala-and-mascarpone–spiked cream, this is a seriously decadent dessert, and there's a healthy hit of cinnamon to add another layer of flavor. It's definitely dinner-party-worthy, and luckily you can make it up to a day ahead. **MAKES 8 TO 10 SERVINGS**

instructions

- **PUT A SAUCEPAN** half-filled with water over high heat and bring to a boil; reduce to a simmer. In a metal bowl large enough to fit over the saucepan, whisk together the egg yolks, 1/3 cup sugar, and 1/4 cup Marsala. Put the bowl over the saucepan of simmering water and whisk constantly until the mixture is light, airy, pale in color, and has reached the ribbon stage (the mixture has thickened enough so that when you lift the whisk and allow the mixture to drizzle back into the bowl, it folds back on itself like a stack of ribbons), about 5 to 8 minutes. Remove from the heat and set aside to cool.

- **IN A MEDIUM BOWL,** whisk together the mascarpone and cinnamon until smooth. Using a handheld mixer, beat the cream, 2 tablespoons of the remaining sugar, and the vanilla on medium-high speed until soft peaks form. Add the mascarpone mixture and beat until medium peaks form, about 1 minute.

- **WHISK** about 1/2 cup of the whipped cream mixture into the egg mixture to lighten it, then fold this back into the cream. Fold in the remaining 3 tablespoons Marsala.

- **IN A MEDIUM BOWL,** combine the coffee, espresso, and remaining 1 tablespoon sugar. Use a serrated knife to cut the donuts in half horizontally, then vertically. Don't be afraid if some of the donuts fall apart a bit. It won't matter once they're layered with the cream. Dunk each piece of donut in the coffee mixture, immersing both sides, until they feel saturated, about 20 seconds. (Discard any extra coffee.)

- **PLACE A LAYER** of coffee-soaked donuts on the bottom of an 8-by-8-inch or 9-by-9-inch square baking dish. Cover with one-third of the cream mixture, spreading evenly, then repeat layering the donuts and cream until you have three layers of each, ending with the cream. Smooth the top and dust with the cocoa powder. Cover the dish with plastic wrap and chill for several hours or overnight to allow the layers and flavors to integrate. Serve cold, dusted with cocoa powder or shaved chocolate.

Pôts de Crème

ingredients

puddings
- 2 CUPS HEAVY CREAM
- 1/4 CUP SUGAR
- 1/4 TEASPOON SEA SALT
- 5 LARGE EGG YOLKS
- 12 OUNCES HIGH-QUALITY (40 TO 49 PERCENT CACAO) MILK CHOCOLATE, FINELY CHOPPED

crisped rice and peanut bark
- 1 CUP WHITE CHOCOLATE CHIPS
- 1/2 CUP CRISPED RICE CEREAL (SUCH AS RICE KRISPIES)
- 1/3 CUP PLUS 1 TABLESPOON TOASTED AND LIGHTLY SALTED SPANISH PEANUTS, CHOPPED

malted whipped cream
- 3/4 CUP HEAVY CREAM
- 1/2 TEASPOON PURE VANILLA EXTRACT
- 2 TABLESPOONS CARNATION MALTED MILK POWDER
- 1 TABLESPOON PLUS 1 1/2 TEASPOONS SUGAR

These rich, silky puddings are outrageously, shamelessly, sinfully good. You have to serve them in small portions; otherwise their richness turns pleasure into pain. They're easy to make, can be made ahead, and are so incredibly impressive that you can whip them up for any occasion. For a fluffy flavor contrast, I top them with malted whipped cream, then add a few shards of crisped rice and Spanish peanut white-chocolate bark. **MAKES 8 SERVINGS**

instructions

- **TO MAKE THE PUDDINGS:** In a medium saucepan, combine the cream, sugar, and salt and bring to a boil over medium heat. Meanwhile, in a medium bowl, whisk the egg yolks. Put the chopped chocolate in a separate large mixing bowl and put a fine-mesh sieve on top.

- **WHEN THE CREAM BEGINS TO BOIL,** remove it from the heat and whisk about 1/4 cup of the hot cream into the egg yolks to temper them. Pour this mixture back into the saucepan with the cream and cook over medium-low heat, stirring constantly, until the custard thickens enough to coat the back of a wooden spoon, 3 to 5 minutes. (To check, dip the spoon in the custard, hold it horizontally, then run your finger across it from the tip to the handle. The custard should be thick enough to not bleed through the line for at least several seconds.)

- **POUR THE CUSTARD** through the fine-mesh sieve over the bowl of chopped chocolate. Let stand for several minutes to melt the chocolate, then whisk together until smooth. Divide the pudding among eight 2- to 3-ounce ramekins. (If you only have 4-ounce ramekins, just fill them about halfway.) Tap each lightly on the counter to remove any air bubbles and refrigerate them until set, several hours. (If you like, you can serve them immediately. They will have the flavor and texture of warm, thick chocolate pudding.)

- **TO MAKE THE BARK:** In a medium microwave-safe bowl, melt the white chocolate chips in the microwave (about four 45-second bursts, stirring between each). Stir in the crisped rice and peanuts. Pour the mixture onto a parchment-lined baking sheet and spread it into a thin layer (about 1/8 inch thick). Chill in the refrigerator until firm, 20 to 30 minutes, then break it up into small shards. (You can make this ahead; just store it in an airtight container at room temperature or in the fridge for up to 1 week.)

continued

- **TO MAKE THE MALTED WHIPPED CREAM:** In the bowl of a stand mixer fitted with a whisk attachment, combine the cream, vanilla, malt powder, and sugar. Beat on medium-high speed until medium-stiff peaks form.
- **LET THE CUSTARDS** stand at room temperature for 20 to 30 minutes (or microwave at 50 percent power for 20 to 30 seconds until slightly soft). Top with a dollop of the malted whipped cream, then insert a shard or two of the bark and serve.

TIPS

- *To quickly chop chocolate into fine pieces, just whiz chunks (about 1 inch or so) of chocolate in a food processor.*
- *Be sure to use high-quality milk chocolate, such as Scharffen Berger or Felchlin Maracaibo 49 percent. There's a lot of mediocre milk chocolate out there, and this recipe depends on the good stuff.*

Black Cow Panna Cotta

Root beer floats (we called them black cows) were one of my favorite summertime desserts when I was growing up in the Midwest, so I decided to give the flavors a grown-up spin in a dessert that would be fantastic for a backyard barbeque. The creamy texture of the panna cotta is truly ethereal. and the root beer drizzle adds a playful touch. I like to garnish these with a freshly baked Oh Snap! Gingersnap Cookie to add a crispy element that ties everything together—and has the added bonus of standing in as a spoon! Even though the components sound fancy, they're quick and easy to make. The only trick is planning ahead, because each needs a few hours to set up. **MAKES 8 SERVINGS**

ingredients

vanilla-bean panna cotta

- 4 CUPS HEAVY CREAM
- ⅓ CUP SUGAR
- ¼ TEASPOON SEA SALT
- 1 VANILLA BEAN
- 3 TABLESPOONS COLD WATER
- 2 TEASPOONS UNFLAVORED POWDERED GELATIN

root beer drizzle

- TWO 12-OUNCE BOTTLES ROOT BEER (SUCH AS HENRY WEINHARD'S DRAUGHT STYLE)
- 2 HEAPING TEASPOONS PEELED, GRATED FRESH GINGER
- ¼ TEASPOON SEA SALT
- 2 TABLESPOONS BLACKSTRAP MOLASSES
- ¼ VANILLA BEAN

- FRESH WHOOP (PAGE 139) FOR GARNISH (OPTIONAL)
- OH SNAP! GINGERSNAP COOKIES (PAGE 49) FOR GARNISH (OPTIONAL)

instructions

- **TO MAKE THE PANNA COTTA:** Place eight 4-ounce ramekins or 4-ounce wide-mouth canning jars in the fridge. (Chilling the cups helps the panna cotta set faster.)

- **IN A MEDIUM SAUCEPAN,** combine the cream, sugar, and salt. Split the vanilla bean lengthwise and scrape out the seeds with the back of a knife. Add to the pan along with the pod and gently bring to a simmer over medium heat, stirring occasionally (do not boil).

- **WHILE THE CREAM IS HEATING,** pour the cold water into a medium bowl and sprinkle the gelatin evenly over the top (you'll be putting some cream in the bowl, so it needs to be big enough). Let stand (don't stir) until the gelatin has absorbed the water, at least 5 minutes.

- **WHEN THE CREAM BEGINS TO SIMMER,** remove it from the heat and remove the vanilla bean pod. (Don't discard it. Rinse, let dry, and save for another use.) Add some of the cream to the bowl of gelatin and whisk until melted. Pour the mixture into the saucepan and whisk thoroughly. Strain the mixture through a fine-mesh sieve into a large liquid measuring cup or bowl with a pouring spout.

- **DIVIDE THE MIXTURE** equally among the chilled ramekins or jars. Refrigerate, uncovered, until set, at least several hours. (It should have the texture of a soft pudding. The panna cottas can be made up to 1 week in advance, but be sure to cover them with plastic wrap if refrigerating for more than a couple of hours; otherwise they'll get dried out.)

- **TO MAKE THE DRIZZLE:** In a medium saucepan, combine the root beer, ginger, salt, and molasses. Split the piece of vanilla bean lengthwise and scrape out the seeds with the back of a knife and add to the pan along with the pod. Bring to a boil over medium heat. Continue to boil until reduced to 3/4 cup, 30 to 40 minutes. Remove from the heat, strain through a fine-mesh sieve, and let cool.

- **TO SERVE,** drizzle each panna cotta with 1 tablespoon of the root beer drizzle and garnish with the whoop and a gingersnap cookie, if desired.

TIP

- *I usually use sheet gelatin (also called leaf gelatin), but it can be hard to find. If you do score some, you'll need about 3½ sheets of 3- by-5-inch sheet gelatin for the panna cotta. To use sheet gelatin, let it rest in a bowl of cold water for 5 to 10 minutes, until soft. (Don't use warm water, or it will melt the gelatin.) Scoop it out of the water with your hands and gently squeeze it to remove the excess water. Then place it directly in the warm liquid and whisk until incorporated.)*

I ❤️ Panna Cotta

What is panna cotta? I get asked this a lot at my cart, and I'm always happy to evangelize about this super-simple yet amazing Italian "cooked cream." Unlike most custards, such as crème caramel, pôt de crème, or crème brûlée, panna cotta is set with gelatin instead of eggs. I love those custards, but the eggs mean they can curdle easily and require a long, slow bake in a water bath. Panna cotta, by contrast, is quick to put together, plays well with all kinds of flavorings, and is practically foolproof.

ingredients

- 1 HEAPING CUP SWEETENED, SHREDDED COCONUT (PREFERABLY ANGEL FLAKE)
- 1/2 CUP ALMONDS
- 3 CUPS UNSWEETENED COCONUT MILK (I USE CHAOKOH BRAND.)
- 4 CUPS HEAVY CREAM
- SCANT 1/2 CUP GRANULATED SUGAR
- 1/8 TEASPOON SEA SALT
- 1 VANILLA BEAN
- 3 TABLESPOONS COLD WATER
- 2 TEASPOONS POWDERED UNFLAVORED GELATIN
- 1/2 TO 1 CUP AUNTI SHIRLEY'S CHOCOLATE SAUCE (PAGE 133)
- FRESH WHOOP (PAGE 139; OPTIONAL)

TIPS

- *If you want to use sheet gelatin, use 3 1/2 sheets of silver gelatin. See page 99 for tips on working with sheet gelatin.*
- *Ungarnished panna cottas will keep in the refrigerator for up to 1 week. Cover each with plastic wrap to keep them from drying out.*

Toasted-Coconut Panna Cotta
WITH AUNTI SHIRLEY'S CHOCOLATE SAUCE

It's not enough to just use coconut milk for this recipe. I steep the milk with toasted, sweetened, shredded coconut to make it truly coconutty. I prefer my panna cottas to be barely set, so they have a silky texture. This means that I use little gelatin and unmolding isn't ideal. But I think panna cotta is much prettier served in a glass cup anyway. At the cart I serve them in little squat-bottomed mason jars, or you can dust off your grandma's fancy vintage glassware and put it to good use. **MAKES 8 SERVINGS**

instructions

- **PREHEAT THE OVEN** to 350°F. Spread the coconut in an even layer on a rimmed baking sheet and toast, stirring occasionally, until most of the shreds are dark golden brown, 5 to 8 minutes. Transfer to a small bowl and let cool. Spread the almonds in an even layer on the baking sheet and toast until fragrant and beginning to color, 5 to 8 minutes. Remove from the oven and turn off the heat. Place eight 4-ounce ramekins or small serving glasses in the fridge. (Chilling the cups helps the panna cotta set faster.)

- **IN A MEDIUM SAUCEPAN,** combine the coconut milk, cream, sugar, salt, and the toasted coconut. Split the vanilla bean lengthwise and scrape out the seeds with the back of a knife. Add to the pan along with the pod and gently bring to a slight simmer over medium heat, stirring occasionally (do not boil).

- **WHILE THE CREAM IS HEATING,** pour the cold water into a small bowl and sprinkle the gelatin evenly over the top. Let stand for at least 5 minutes.

- **WHEN THE CREAM HAS BEGUN TO SIMMER,** remove it from the heat and strain it through a fine-mesh sieve into a large measuring cup or bowl with a spout. Use a spatula to gently press the coconut against the sieve to force out all the liquid. Discard the solids and vanilla bean pod. Add the softened gelatin to the hot cream and whisk until incorporated. (You shouldn't see any bits of solid gelatin.)

- **DIVIDE THE MIXTURE** equally among the chilled cups (do not cover with plastic wrap) and refrigerate until set, least 3 hours. (It should have the texture of a soft pudding.) Serve with 1 1/2 to 2 tablespoons chocolate sauce, a dollop of whoop and a sprinkling of toasted, chopped almonds.

lemon cream

- 1 RECIPE LUSCIOUS LEMON CURD, COOLED (PAGE 135)
- 2 TABLESPOONS HEAVY CREAM

gingersnap crunch

- 1 CUP FINELY GROUND GINGERSNAP COOKIES (ABOUT 15-20 SMALL CRISPY COOKIES)
- 1/8 TEASPOON SEA SALT
- 2 TABLESPOONS UNSALTED BUTTER, MELTED

Lemon Puddin' Pops

Lemon curd doesn't last long in my kitchen, but one day I actually did have some extra lingering in the fridge, and I wondered what would happen if I froze it. I figured I had a fifty-fifty chance of ending up with something icy and weird or something really awesome. I got lucky, because the result was amazing—silky, smooth frozen lemon custard that just melts in your mouth. It was just begging to be turned into a pudding pop, so I froze some more in little vintage gelatin molds and rolled the pops in crushed gingersnaps. Hot damn! This is such a fun dessert to serve in the summertime, when you crave something cool and creamy but want something with a little more personality than a scoop of ice cream. You can even tuck some fresh market berries into the molds for added pops of color and texture. Lemon and raspberry is a particularly happy match. Try serving them with some Fresh Whoop (page 139) on the side and experiment with dipping options, like toasted coconut and finely chopped toasted nuts. **MAKES 6 TO 8 SERVINGS**

instructions

- **TO MAKE THE LEMON CREAM:** Place six to eight gelatin molds or popsicle molds in the freezer to chill. (The amount of pops this recipe makes depends on the size of your molds. I get eight pops using my small, 3-ounce vintage gelatin molds, or six when I use standard 4-ounce popsicle molds.)

- **IN THE BOWL OF A BLENDER OR FOOD PROCESSOR,** purée the cooled lemon curd for 30 seconds. Add the heavy cream 1 tablespoon at a time, blending for a few seconds between each addition. (Once the curd has been whipped it will turn a lovely pale yellow and it will have the most amazing lighter-than-air texture. I highly recommend this technique even if you're serving the lemon curd straight up.) Transfer the mixture to a 4-cup liquid measuring cup with a spout and pour into the pre-chilled molds. (If you want to add berries place a few at the bottom of the molds, then tuck a few more in once the molds have been filled, though you might need a couple more molds.)

- **TAP OUT ANY EXCESS AIR BUBBLES,** insert popsicle sticks, and return to the freezer to chill for at least 2 hours or overnight. They need to be completely frozen before unmolding.

continued

- **TO MAKE THE GINGERSNAP CRUNCH:** Preheat oven to 350°F. In a small bowl, combine the ground gingersnaps and salt. Pour in the melted butter and mix until the crumbs are evenly moistened. Spread the crumbs on a rimmed baking sheet and toast for 5 to 7 minutes, until beginning to crisp. Set aside to cool.

- **PLACE A WARM WASHCLOTH** on the outside of the molds for a few seconds to help loosen the frozen curd. Holding the stick, invert the molds and gently lift off. Roll the popsicles in the gingersnap crunch and serve immediately.

POP CULTURE

Frozen Yogurt

Along with stirrup pants, slouchy boots, and off-the-shoulder shirts, fro-yo has been resurrected from the '80s. I'm all for it. I love how tart and refreshing true frozen yogurt is. It's perfect on a hot day with fresh berries, or use it to make an ice-cream sandwich with Oh Snap! Gingersnap Cookies (page 49). It even makes an excellent ginger ale float with a dash of celery bitters. **MAKES 1 QUART**

instructions

- **SPLIT THE PIECE OF VANILLA BEAN** lengthwise and scrape out the seeds with the back of a knife. Add to the bowl of a blender (save the pod for another use). Chop the apple (with skin on) into 1-inch pieces. Add the apple, sorbet syrup, yogurt, lime zest and juice, and salt to the bowl and blend on medium-high speed until smooth, 1 to 2 minutes.

- **STRAIN THE MIXTURE** through a fine-mesh sieve into a bowl, making sure to press on the solids to force out all the liquid; discard the solids. Refrigerate the mixture until very cold. (The colder the base, the faster it will churn. To speed things up, you can nestle the bowl into a larger bowl filled with water and ice and refrigerate.)

- **POUR THE CHILLED FROZEN YOGURT BASE** into an ice-cream maker and freeze according to the manufacturer's instructions. (If everything is super-cold, it should take 20 to 25 minutes. The frozen yogurt will thicken and ball up on the attachment. Don't over-churn, or you will get a grainy, hard texture.)

- **TRANSFER TO AN AIRTIGHT CONTAINER,** place plastic wrap directly on the surface, and freeze for several hours until firm enough to scoop.

Sorbet Syrup #1

MAKES ABOUT 1⅔ CUPS

- ¾ CUP WATER
- ½ CUP SUGAR
- ¾ CUP LIGHT CORN SYRUP

- **IN A MEDIUM SAUCEPAN,** combine the water, sugar, and light corn syrup and bring to a rolling boil over high heat. Continue to boil for 2 minutes, remove from the heat, and transfer to a metal bowl. Chill in an ice bath or in the refrigerator until very cold before using.

ingredients

- 5 SMALL- TO MEDIUM-SIZE VERY RIPE BANANAS
- 5 TABLESPOONS FLAVORFUL HONEY, SUCH AS MEADOWFOAM
- 1/8 TEASPOON SEA SALT, PLUS 1/4 TEASPOON
- 2 1/2 CUPS COLD HEAVY CREAM
- 1/4 TEASPOON FRESHLY GRATED NUTMEG
- 1 TEASPOON VANILLA EXTRACT (OR SEEDS FROM 1/2 VANILLA BEAN)

Roasted~Banana
ICE CREAM

Since bananas are so rich and creamy on their own, you can use them in ice cream and skip the hassle of cooking up an eggy custard base. Not only does that save time, but it also imparts an even stronger banana flavor. Roasting the bananas with honey caramelizes them and brings out their sweetness. After that, you just whiz everything up in a food processor and chill. So easy and so good. This ice cream is delicious in a sundae with Aunti Shirley's Chocolate Sauce (page 133) and cinnamon-spiked whipped cream, and it makes an incredible ice-cream sandwich with the Hazelnibbies (page 59). It's like having banana-bread ice cream. **MAKES 1 QUART**

instructions

- **PREHEAT THE OVEN** to 375°F. Line a rimmed baking sheet with parchment paper or a Silpat. Place a large bowl in the fridge or freezer.

- **CUT THE UNPEELED BANANAS** in half lengthwise through their peels (leave in their peels). Place cut-side up on the prepared baking sheet and drizzle them with 2 tablespoons of the honey. Sprinkle with the 1/8 teaspoon sea salt. Roast on the middle rack until deeply colored, fragrant, and very soft, 20 to 25 minutes. The kitchen will take on a lovely roasted-banana aroma. Let cool completely.

- **WHEN COOL,** scoop the banana flesh out of the peels and into the bowl of a food processor or blender. Puree until very smooth. Add the cream, nutmeg, remaining 1/4 teaspoon salt, vanilla, and remaining 3 tablespoons honey. Pulse several times just until smooth. (The mixture will be on the thick side. Make sure not to overmix, or you will end up with banana whipped cream!) Transfer the mixture to the chilled metal bowl, place plastic wrap directly on the surface, and refrigerate until very cold, at least 1 hour.

- **FREEZE THE MIXTURE** in an ice-cream maker according to the manufacturer's instructions, 20 to 25 minutes. Transfer to an airtight container, place plastic wrap directly on the surface, and freeze until firm enough to scoop, at least another hour. (If the ice cream becomes too firm to scoop, let it soften a bit for 5 minutes at room temperature before serving, or run your ice-cream scoop under hot water before using.)

- 1½ CUPS SUGAR
- 8 OUNCES REGULAR CREAM CHEESE, AT ROOM TEMPERATURE (I PREFER PHILADELPHIA BRAND)
- ⅛ TEASPOON SEA SALT
- 2 LARGE EGGS
- 1½ CUPS WHOLE MILK
- 3 CUPS HEAVY CREAM
- 2 TO 2½ TEASPOONS CREAM SODA EXTRACT (SEE TIP)

TIP

- *Taste the custard as you go; you might want a lighter cream soda flavor, or you might want more. The flavor will mellow after the ice cream has been churned. Still, don't get too crazy—anything over 2½ teaspoons is too much—because it's strong and can impart a bitter aftertaste. I use Old Fashioned Homebrew brand.*

Cream Soda

ICE CREAM

This cream cheese ice-cream base is fantastic. It is super-rich, has a wonderfully silky texture, and it doesn't get rock hard when you freeze it. It's adapted from a recipe in *The Ultimate Ice Cream Book* by Bruce Weinstein, a great book I've used often through the years. The ice cream can be flavored dozens of ways, but cream soda extract is one of my favorites. It's fun and different, and the flavor goes with lots of my desserts. Try this in an ice-cream sandwich with Oh Snap! Gingersnap Cookies (page 49) or Giddyup Cookies (page 48). Keep in mind, the extract is very strong—like burn-your-tongue-off strong—so use a very light hand, and don't taste it on its own unless you're looking for pain. **MAKES ABOUT 1½ QUARTS**

instructions

- **IN THE BOWL OF A STAND MIXER** fitted with a paddle attachment, combine the sugar, cream cheese, and salt. Beat on medium-high speed until smooth, 1 to 2 minutes. Scrape down the sides of the bowl. With the mixer on medium speed, add the eggs, one at a time, beating well after each addition. Continue beating until smooth and glossy, 1 to 2 minutes.

- **COMBINE THE MILK AND CREAM** in a medium saucepan and bring to a slight boil over medium-high heat, stirring occasionally. Remove from the heat. Whisk about ½ cup of the hot cream into the cheese mixture to temper it, then whisk this mixture back into the saucepan. Cook over medium-low heat, stirring often with a wooden spoon, until the custard thickens (run your finger along the back of the spoon; the custard shouldn't bleed into the line for several seconds), 5 to 8 minutes.

- **REMOVE FROM THE HEAT** and strain the custard into a metal bowl. Nestle the bowl in a larger bowl filled with ice and a little water. Let the mixture cool, stirring occasionally, until lukewarm, about 15 minutes. Stir in the cream soda extract.

- **REFRIGERATE UNTIL THE CUSTARD IS COLD,** at least several hours. Give it a good stir, then freeze in two batches in an ice-cream maker according to the manufacturer's instructions, 20 to 25 minutes. Transfer to an airtight container, put plastic wrap directly on the surface, and freeze until firm enough to scoop, at least several hours.

Cherry Lambic Sorbet

ingredients

- 1/2 CUP LINDEMAN'S KRIEK CHERRY LAMBIC BEER, PLUS 2 TABLESPOONS
- 3 CUPS (ABOUT 1 POUND) FIRMLY PACKED FRESH OR FROZEN PITTED CHERRIES
- JUICE OF 1 LEMON
- 1 1/2 CUPS SORBET SYRUP #2 (RECIPE FOLLOWS)
- 1/8 TEASPOON SEA SALT

TIP

- *Just as ovens can vary in efficiency, so can freezers. It might take longer for your sorbets and ice creams to firm up than it takes for mine. Just be patient. If you're planning on serving one as a dinner party dessert, your best bet is to start it the day before. This way you give the mixture time to chill down properly before churning, and you give the churned ice cream or sorbet time to firm up before serving.*

Sour, dry Belgian lambics are just bursting with flavor, so I love incorporating them into desserts. For this sorbet, inspired by a recipe in *The Ciao Bella Book of Gelato and Sorbetto*, I use both cherry lambic and a pound of fresh cherries for a double wallop of fruit flavor. It has a beautifully smooth easy-to-scoop texture and would make an amazing float with spicy ginger ale. After measuring out the half cup of beer to reduce on the stove, you'll be tempted to drink the rest, but don't drink it all! I know it's hard to resist, but you need a few tablespoons of unboiled lambic to brighten the sorbet's flavor. **MAKES 1 QUART**

instructions

- **IN A SMALL SAUCEPAN,** bring the 1/2 cup of lambic beer to a boil over medium-high heat and continue to boil until slightly thickened, about 1 minute. Remove from heat and let cool.

- **IN THE BOWL OF A FOOD PROCESSOR** or blender, purée the cherries, lemon juice, sorbet syrup, and salt. Strain through a fine-mesh sieve into a medium mixing bowl, pressing on the solids to squeeze all the juices out. Stir in the reduced lambic and the remaining 2 tablespoons fresh lambic.

- **CHILL FOR AT LEAST 3 HOURS** or overnight. Freeze the mixture in an ice-cream maker according to the manufacturer's instructions, 15 to 20 minutes. Transfer the sorbet to an airtight container, put plastic wrap directly on the surface, and freeze overnight, or until firm enough to scoop, (because of the alcohol it'll take longer to freeze).

Sorbet Syrup #2

MAKES ABOUT 2 1/2 CUPS

- 1 1/4 CUPS SUGAR
- 2 CUPS WATER

- **IN A MEDIUM SAUCEPAN,** combine the sugar and water and bring to a boil over high heat. Continue to boil for 2 minutes, remove from the heat, and transfer to a metal bowl. Chill in an ice bath or in the refrigerator until very cold before using.

TIPS

- *If you want to serve this scooped like a sorbet, you can freeze the slushy in an airtight container for several hours until firm enough to scoop.*

- *Nigori Sake has a cloudy, milky appearance because it's unfiltered. It's the sweetest of all the sakes and has a fruity/floral nose and a mild flavor that make it great to use in or pair with desserts. I like Sayuri brand; it comes in a pretty pink bottle, and you can find it at supermarkets like Whole Foods. Make sure to shake the bottle a couple of times before serving or using to distribute the sediment that has settled.*

- *If you use Meyer lemons for the lemon juice, don't waste all that beautiful zest! Zest the lemons into a small, airtight container or onto a piece of plastic wrap, cover or fold up, and freeze for later use.*

Meyer Lemon-Sake Slushy

Slurpees have their place—but not in the hands of anyone over the age of twenty. All those artificial flavors and colors and that saccharine sweetness just get harder to appreciate the older you are. That being said, the texture never gets old, so I've created a distinctly grown-up version using unfiltered Nigori sake and Meyer lemon juice. The sake has a delicate, yeasty sweetness that pairs particularly well with the bright, milder-flavored, slightly floral Meyer lemon juice. Although the slushy takes a little elbow grease to make, it's way worth it. **MAKES 6 TO 8 SERVINGS, 1½ QUARTS**

instructions

- **CHILL A 9-BY-13-INCH GLASS BAKING DISH** in the freezer. In a large metal bowl, combine the sugar, lemon zest, and boiling water. Stir to dissolve the sugar and let cool for a few minutes before adding the lemon juice and sake. Stir to combine, then pour the mixture into the chilled dish and freeze for 2 hours.

- **USE A WIRE WHISK OR FORK** to mash and scrape the partially frozen mixture, breaking it up completely. Return it to the freezer for 1 hour and then repeat the mashing and scraping. Freeze again for another hour and scrape again. It will take on a flaked texture.

- **WHEN THE MIXTURE IS FLAKED** and frozen (not soupy or slushy), transfer it to a 10- to 14-cup food processor and pulse until smooth and slushy, 20 to 30 seconds. If you don't have a food processor, you can purée the mixture in batches in a blender. If it's hard to blend in the blender, just give it a good stir and continue to blend.

- **SERVE IN TALL ICE-COLD GLASSES** and garnish each with a fresh Meyer lemon wedge.

sorbet

- 1½ CUPS WATER
- 1¾ CUPS GRANULATED SUGAR
- GRATED ZEST OF 1 ORANGE OR TANGERINE
- GRATED ZEST OF 1 MEYER LEMON
- ⅛ TEASPOON SEA SALT
- ONE 750-ML BOTTLE BRUT CHAMPAGNE OR SPARKLING WINE, SUCH AS CAVA
- 1 VANILLA BEAN (I RECOMMEND TAHITIAN FOR THIS)

strawberries

- 1½ TO 2 PINTS FRESH, RIPE, SWEET STRAWBERRIES, HULLED AND SLICED
- ⅛ TEASPOON SEA SALT
- JUICE OF ½ MEYER LEMON
- 2 TABLESPOONS SUPERFINE SUGAR, OR MORE TO TASTE

TIPS

- *There's so much alcohol in the sorbet that it takes a long time to freeze. It will look slightly slushy after churning, so move fast and have your storage container already chilled when you're done churning to keep it good and cold.*

- *Yes, I salt my strawberries. Am I a salt freak? Maybe. But that doesn't mean it's not a good idea. Just a pinch of salt will bring out and support the fruit's flavor without making it taste salty. Trust me.*

Champagne and Strawberries

This refreshing, light sorbet is intoxicating but not in *that* way. It's the vanilla bean and citrus zest that give it a beguiling floral undertone, especially if you use Meyer lemons and Tahitian vanilla beans, both of which have floral notes. This was one of my favorite desserts that pastry chef Della Gossett made during my time at Trio. Drop a couple scoops in a vintage coupe dish, scatter fresh strawberries on top (or any other berries or stone fruit), and you have a simple but very stylish dessert. It's also fantastic afloat in freshly squeezed orange juice for a reverse Mimosa or in the Fizzy Lifting Drink (page 123). **MAKES 6 TO 8 SERVINGS**

instructions

- **TO MAKE THE SORBET:** In a large saucepan, combine the water, sugar, orange zest, lemon zest, salt, and champagne. Split the vanilla bean lengthwise and scrape out the seeds with the back of a knife. Add to the pan along with the pod and bring to a boil over medium-high heat, stirring to dissolve the sugar. Continue boiling for about 1 minute.

- **REMOVE FROM THE HEAT** and remove the vanilla bean pod. (Don't discard the pod. Rinse, let dry, and save for another use.) Strain the mixture through a fine-mesh sieve into a metal bowl. Put the bowl in a larger bowl filled with ice and water. Put the whole thing, ice bath and all, into the refrigerator to chill until cold, 3 to 4 hours. (If you're working ahead, you can transfer the mixture to an airtight container and chill overnight.)

- **PLACE AN AIRTIGHT CONTAINER** large enough to store the churned sorbet in the freezer to chill before filling. Freeze the mixture in an ice-cream maker according to the manufacturer's instructions, 20 to 25 minutes. Immediately transfer the sorbet to the chilled container. Place plastic wrap directly on the surface, cover, and freeze for several hours or overnight until firm enough to scoop.

- **TO PREPARE THE STRAWBERRIES:** In a medium bowl, combine the strawberries, salt, lemon juice, and sugar and toss to coat. Taste and add more sugar if necessary. Let macerate until the berries release some of their juice, at least 20 to 25 minutes.

- **PLACE A COUPLE SCOOPS** of sorbet in the bottom of a small bowl or chilled stemmed glass. Spoon some of the macerated strawberries on top and serve.

6

SIPS, SLURPS, and MIDNIGHT MUNCHIES

Put down the fork. This is no place for cutlery. Everyone needs to have a few good go-to nibbles in his or her bag of tricks, things like sexy truffled popcorn and spicy candied nuts that you can munch on during movies or set out at a cocktail party. And it would be a crime to forget about the drinks to sip along with them. I've had drinks on my menu from the very beginning, because some treats really are best in liquid form. Here are a few of my favorite and most popular recipes.

ingredients

- 8 OUNCES (2 STICKS) UNSALTED BUTTER
- 1 CUP SUGAR
- 1/4 CUP WATER
- 1/2 TEASPOON SEA SALT
- 3 TABLESPOONS BLACK SESAME SEEDS
- 3 TABLESPOONS WHITE SESAME SEEDS

BLACK-AND-WHITE
Sesame Brittle

Fast, easy, cheap, and yet impressive, this confection makes the best DIY last-minute gift. Forgot your friend's birthday? Too embarrassed to bring that bottle of Two-Buck Chuck to the dinner party? Make a batch of this candy and soak up the praise. It has a light and crunchy texture that doesn't get stuck in your teeth, and the contrasting black and white sesame seeds give it a nutty and slightly bitter flavor that's a welcome change from the usual peanuts. **MAKES ABOUT 1½ POUNDS**

instructions

- **LINE A LARGE BAKING SHEET** with parchment paper. In a medium, heavy-bottomed pot, combine the butter, sugar, water, and salt and cook over medium-high heat, swirling the pot, until the mixture reaches 260°F on a candy thermometer. Add the seeds and continue cooking, stirring constantly, until the mixture reaches 350°F, or until the sugar takes on a dark golden brown color.

- **REMOVE FROM THE HEAT** and immediately pour the mixture into the prepared pan, spreading it into an even layer about 1/4 inch thick. Set aside to cool until firm.

- **ONCE THE BRITTLE HAS SET,** break it into pieces and serve in a candy dish, over ice cream, or dipped in bittersweet chocolate.

Popcorn

ingredients

- ½ CUP POPCORN KERNELS
- 3 TABLESPOONS OLIVE OR VEGETABLE OIL (IF POPPING ON THE STOVE)
- 1 TABLESPOON PLUS 1 TEASPOON TRUFFLE OIL OR TRUFFLE SEA SALT, PLUS MORE TO TASTE (OPTIONAL)
- ½ TEASPOON FLAKY SEA SALT, SUCH AS FLEUR DE SEL OR MALDON, PLUS MORE TO TASTE
- A COUPLE OF GRINDS OF PEPPER
- 1 TO 2 TABLESPOONS FLAVORFUL HONEY, SUCH AS MEADOWFOAM OR CHESTNUT, PLUS MORE TO TASTE

Most people think butter or caramel when they think of popcorn. But why limit yourself? It's corn, after all, so it can actually go with just about anything. Musky, rich truffle oil and bold honey make this a particularly grown-up version that's as welcome on movie night as it is at a cocktail party. **MAKES ABOUT 8 CUPS**

instructions

- **PLACE A LARGE,** heavy-lidded pot (like a stockpot or Dutch oven) over medium heat. Add the vegetable oil and the popcorn kernels, cover, and shake the pot back and forth until the kernels have popped. (You may have to do this in batches if you only have a small pot.) Or, pop the popcorn using an air popper according to the manufacturer's instructions.

- **TRANSFER THE POPCORN** to a large mixing bowl. (It needs to be large enough to allow you to really toss the popcorn around. If you don't have a large bowl, toss the popcorn in batches.) Drizzle with the truffle oil while tossing the popcorn. Add the salt and toss to distribute. Drizzle in the honey while tossing. Keep tossing until the popcorn seems evenly flavored. Add the pepper and more truffle oil, salt, or honey (if desired).

ingredients

- 4 CUPS (1 POUND) WHOLE PECANS
- 2 TABLESPOONS UNSALTED BUTTER
- 3 TO 4 TABLESPOONS GRADE B MAPLE SYRUP
- 1/2 TEASPOON PURE VANILLA EXTRACT OR VANILLA PASTE
- 1/4 CUP PLUS 2 TABLESPOONS PACKED DARK BROWN SUGAR
- 1 1/4 TO 1 1/2 TEASPOONS CAYENNE PEPPER (USE MORE IF YOU LIKE IT SPICY!)
- 1 1/4 TEASPOONS SEA SALT
- A COUPLE SPLASHES OF TABASCO SAUCE FOR MORE KICK (OPTIONAL)

Spicy Nutz

Once you make your own candied nuts, you'll never, ever be willing to pay for them again. Those tiny, expensive bags of stale, sugary nuts just can't compare with what you can make fresh for half the price. This recipe was inspired by the spicy nuts I snack on at Bunk Bar in Portland. They're amazing in a mixed salad, paired with a cheese plate, or just eaten on their own. The sweet, crunchy caramel, toasty nuts, and pop of spice work so well together, it's hard not to consume an entire batch in one sitting. So make sure you invite some friends over to share in the gluttony.

MAKES 4 CUPS

instructions

- **PREHEAT THE OVEN** to 350°F. Spread the nuts in an even layer on a rimmed baking sheet and toast until fragrant and beginning to color, 10 to 15 minutes.

- **MEANWHILE, MELT THE BUTTER** in a small saucepan or in the microwave. Stir in the maple syrup and vanilla.

- **TRANSFER THE TOASTED NUTS** to a large bowl. Add the brown sugar, cayenne, and salt and toss to combine. Drizzle with the butter mixture and toss to coat. Taste and add Tabasco (if using).

- **LINE A BAKING SHEET** with parchment paper or a Silpat. Spread the coated nuts in an even layer on the prepared sheet and bake for 10 to 12 minutes, stirring once during the last five minutes. The pecans will take on a rich, dark, caramelized color and look slightly bubbled from the melting sugar.

- **LET COOL** slightly in the pan on a wire rack before breaking up into pieces.

Vanilla

I use vanilla in a lot of my recipes. It rounds out and supports the other flavors, providing welcome depth that makes everything taste better. For a lot of recipes, pure vanilla extract works perfectly (just don't use the imitation stuff). But you should be picky about which extract you buy.

Extract is made by macerating vanilla beans in a water and alcohol solution, then aging it. And, like everything, some producers do this better than others: They use better beans, steep them longer, age the solution longer, and don't add colorings or additives. I like extracts from Penzeys or The Spice House because they're rich and nuanced.

Some recipes, however, are best made with vanilla beans. Sometimes it's an aesthetic choice—you want to see those lovely little black bean specks–sometimes it's because you need to steep or infuse something with the bean's stronger flavor—like when you're making custards or browned butter.

I prefer Tahitian vanilla because it has wonderful floral notes, but Bourbon vanilla, which has a rich, mellow flavor, is great, too. When you're shopping for whole beans, make sure they're plump and moist, not dry or wizened. They should be stored in an airtight container in a cool, dark place. Although you can find them at the supermarket, they're usually more expensive there. You can get more bang for your buck if you buy beans in bulk from a reputable online retailer.

Vanilla beans are so expensive because they're labor intensive to produce. The beans are the seed pods of a particular variety of orchid, and they must be carefully cured over the course of several months before they're ready for market. So don't toss out that vanilla bean pod even after it has been infused in milk or cream. There's still a lot of goodness in there that you don't want to waste. Just rinse it and let it air-dry. Then you can either pack it in a canister of sugar to make vanilla sugar, or grind it up in a spice grinder to make vanilla powder that you can add to desserts. Any pods that haven't been infused in cream can be used to bump up the flavor of your store-bought vanilla extract. Or use them to make your own: Pack them in a jar (preferably with some whole beans, too), cover with vodka, and let steep for several months. For a never-ending supply, top off with more vodka as you use up the extract (or in the case of vanilla sugar, top off the canister with more sugar), and keep adding used pods whenever you have them.

ingredients

- 9 OUNCES BITTERSWEET CHOCO-LATE (LIKE FELCHLIN CRU HACIENDA, VALRHONA MANJARI, SCHARFFEN BERGER, OR GREEN & BLACK'S)
- 1 CUP HEAVY CREAM
- 1/4 TEASPOON SEA SALT, SUCH AS FLEUR DE SEL OR SMOKED SEA SALT (WHICH WOULD BE FAB WITH THE TOBACCO NOTES FROM THE CHOCO-LATE AND THE TAWNY PORT)
- 4 TO 5 TABLESPOONS DON PX SHERRY OR GOOD TAWNY PORT, OR MORE
- 1 CUP DUTCH-PROCESS COCOA

The Don

I have a serious obsession with Don PX, a rich, sweet dessert sherry made with dried Pedro Ximénez grapes. Splashing it into my bittersweet truffle base was a no-brainer, as the fruity sweetness of the sherry is dynamite with the silky, melt-in-your-mouth chocolate. I tend to gravitate toward higher-quality chocolates with 70 percent or more cocoa solids. The flavor is more intense, and, depending on the origin of the beans, you get great undertones of nuts, citrus, or tropical fruit, especially when you garnish the truffles with a sprinkle of sea salt. Give your piggy bank an extra shake or go through the couch once more for change; if you're going to make these truffles you should splurge. **MAKES ABOUT 30 TRUFFLES**

instructions

- **USE A SERRATED KNIFE** to chop the chocolate into small chunks. (A serrated knife seems to work best, and chopping the chocolate into small pieces helps it melt more quickly and evenly.) Place the chopped chocolate in a medium heat-safe bowl, such as glass or stainless steel.

- **IN A SMALL SAUCEPAN,** bring the cream and salt just to a simmer over medium-low heat. Remove from the heat and let cool for 1 minute. Pour the cream into the bowl of chocolate. Let stand for several minutes before mixing with a spatula until the chocolate takes on a lovely glossy appearance. (If for some reason the chopped chocolate doesn't melt all the way, put the bowl over a pot of barely simmering water to help melt any stragglers. Be very careful not to burn your chocolate.) Remove from the heat and stir in the sherry, tasting as you go until the mixture tastes right to you.

- **LET THE GANACHE COOL SLIGHTLY** before placing plastic wrap directly on the surface and refrigerating for several hours until firm enough to scoop.

- **TO FORM THE TRUFFLES,** use a melon baller or very small ice-cream scoop to scoop out 1-tablespoon portions of the ganache. (These tools will produce evenly sized truffles, but if you don't have them, just use a tablespoon.) Roll the ganache between your palms to round out the shape. Place the shaped truffles on a parchment-lined baking sheet. When the tray is full, put it in the refrigerator to cool down the chocolate and firm it up again, about 20 minutes.

- **SIFT THE COCOA POWDER** into a wide shallow bowl. Place several truffles in the bowl and swirl the bowl to roll them around until they are completely coated with cocoa. Scoop them up into your palm and shake gently to sift the excess cocoa between your fingers. Serve immediately on a dish or in little paper truffle cups, or store in an airtight container in the fridge for up to 1 week.

continued

Sea Salt

:::

There are hundreds of fancy sea salts out there for a reason: They all taste slightly different. The minerals in the seawater and the harvesting techniques can all contribute to salts with slightly different flavors, colors, and textures. Then, of course, there are the flavored salts and smoked salts, which range from subtle to intense.

With all this selection out there, it makes no sense to use ordinary, processed table salt in your cooking. It's like using old, dry herbs instead of fresh: One whispers, the other sings. True, sea salt can get pricey, so I buy it in bulk from natural food stores that have a good bulk selection. For the fancier salts, a little goes a long way, so I just buy small jars and use them judiciously. I love to stop by The Meadow, a Portland salt shop, to pick up little bottles of exotic salts to play with. It's one of my more affordable addictions.

To get your salt fetish going, try serving these truffles with a flight of at least three different kinds of salt—Japanese plum salt is especially good. If you want to get really fancy, serve them on a pink Himalayan salt block, which you can reuse as a cooking plank.

VARIATION:

- **IF YOU OMIT THE SHERRY,** you have an incredibly useful truffle base that you can flavor all kinds of ways. Try adding different flavors of spirits or ground spices. Instead of cocoa powder, you can roll these truffles in other tasty things, such as toasted coconut or chopped toasted pecans.

TIPS

- *Truffles should be served like a good piece of cheese: at room temperature. This will allow you to experience the full flavor and texture explosion that is about to set off in your mouth. For an extra side of awesomeness, sprinkle a few grains of salt on top of each truffle, or serve them with a small dish of fleur de sel. Chocolate and salt are a match made in heaven.*
- *Don't forget to save your cocoa powder. Just sift out any chocolate remnants and store it in an airtight container.*
- *Don PX has this amazingly complex flavor, with lots of raisin notes—but in a good way. If you can splurge, get the Don PX Gran Reserva '82. Just save the rest for special occasions or to sip by the fire. A little goes a long way.*
- *I particularly love Felchlin Cru Hacienda 74 percent for these truffles, because it has rich flavors of citrus, mild tobacco, and tropical banana, plus an incredible mouthfeel that just melts away. But feel free to find your own favorite, just don't skimp. There are plenty of specialty stores and chocolatiers that can help you select a good-quality chocolate for this recipe.*

Fizzy Lifting Drink

ingredients

- ICE
- 1 CUP GINGER ALE
- ½ TO 1 TEASPOON PEELED AND GRATED FRESH GINGER
- 1 TO 2 TABLESPOONS JAPANESE PLUM DRINKING VINEGAR (CALLED *UME*), OR MORE TO TASTE

I know what you're thinking: Who in their right mind would drink vinegar? But trust me; this is a fruity, thirst-quenching, refresher of a drink that is not at all mouth puckering. I love to serve this potion in a mason jar with some fresh raspberries or blackberries to liven it up even more. **MAKES 1 SERVING**

instructions

- **FILL A TALL GLASS** halfway with ice. Pour in ginger ale. Add fresh ginger and top with the plum vinegar. Mix with a long-handled spoon and voilà!

VARIATIONS:

Rated R

- **ADD A SPLASH** (2 or 3 ounces) of good-quality chilled vodka or a couple scoops of champagne sorbet (page 111) or Cherry Lambic Sorbet (page 109).

PG

- **ADD A SCOOP** of lemon sorbet.

- **P.S.:** Take it from me, this drink is great for hangovers. It's a good way to get hydrated, and it settles the tummy. It's what I prescribe whenever I see a customer shuffling over to my cart, looking a bit queasy.

TIP

- *Drinking vinegars, which are very popular in Japan and are thought to promote good health, are available in many flavors at bigger Asian food markets. Just ask specifically for drinking vinegar. Or you can buy them online from sources like AsianFoodGrocer.com. They're not as acidic as regular vinegar, so make sure to store them in the fridge once opened. A word of advice: Stay away from the lemon and strawberry flavors; they taste artificial.*

- 1 TEASPOON CRÈME DE CASSIS LIQUEUR, SUCH AS CLEAR CREEK CASSIS LIQUEUR
- SPARKLING OR STILL ROSÉ

Sexy Kir

Kir royales are one of my favorite things to sip at this sweet little Portland wine bar called Kir. Now, I'll admit that there is a special kind of awesomeness to sitting in a wine bar with your name on it, drinking a drink with your name on it, but both would get pretty old pretty darn quick if they weren't awesome all on their own. And they are. Kir is owned by Amalie Roberts, a friend of mine who has seemingly infinite wisdom about wine, especially rosé, which is how I got turned on to these gorgeous kir royales, which are made with sparkling rosé instead of Champagne. Amalie highly recommends Oregon-made Clear Creek cassis because it's very concentrated in flavor and less sweet. She's also careful to pair the cassis with a wine that is higher in acid to balance out the sweetness of the berry liqueur.

MAKES 1 SERVING

instructions

- **SPOON THE CASSIS** into the bottom of a Champagne flute or coupe if using sparkling wine or the bottom of a wineglass if using still wine. Top with wine and enjoy!

TIPS

- *For a sparkling rosé, Amalie recommends O. Rosal Cava. It has a dry, bright, crisp, clean finish with floral and cranberry notes. For a still rosé, she recommends Rochette Beaujolais Rosé. It comes from the southern region of Burgundy and has a pleasant creaminess, rich flavor, and nice herbal notes on the finish.*

- *If you ever find yourself in Portland, you must pay a visit to Kir. It's like walking into a friend's tiny, cozy little home. Pull up a chair and drink some thoughtfully chosen wine, eat some lovingly crafted food, and hopefully strike up a conversation with someone new. The place is so small that getting to know your neighbor is highly likely—and what makes the whole experience even more memorable.*

Malted Hot Chocolate

ingredients

- 1½ CUPS WHOLE MILK
- 2 HEAPING TABLESPOONS ORIGINAL OVALTINE POWDER
- 2 HEAPING TABLESPOONS GRATED HIGH-QUALITY MILK CHOCOLATE (I LIKE TO USE THE FELCHLIN MARACAIBO 49 PERCENT MILK CHOCOLATE.)
- FRESH WHOOP (PAGE 139) FOR GARNISH
- SMOKED SEA SALT FOR GARNISH (I USE GUAVA-WOOD-SMOKED SEA SALT FROM HAWAII)

Some kids grew up with Hershey's, but I grew up with Ovaltine. I think it was supposed to be somewhat nutritious, which is why my mom had it around, but all I cared about was that yummy malty flavor. I remember one cold Chicago winter when I was a teenager, my friends and I went outside to "go for a walk," but we were really out getting high. When we got back, my mom was standing in the doorway with a tray of steaming mugs of Ovaltine and cookies. It was a genuine Hallmark moment, except for the getting high part. I can still see my friends looking at me with their glazed eyes and telling me I had the best mom in the world. They were right, which made me feel like a total shit. If only she knew what I was doing out there! I've carried on her loving tradition at the cart, updating it with nuances like high-quality milk chocolate, fresh whipped cream, and smoked sea salt. It's a delicious, warming treat—even when you're not cross-eyed! **MAKES 1 SERVING**

instructions

- **IN A SMALL NONREACTIVE SAUCEPAN,** heat the milk over medium heat until steaming. Stir in the Ovaltine and chocolate until thoroughly blended.
- **POUR INTO A LARGE MUG** and top with whoop and a light sprinkle of smoked sea salt.

TIP
- *Milk can have nuances, both good and bad, depending on the brand, what it's packaged in, how long it's been around, what the cows ate, and so on. I say if you're going to drink a big mug of milk, make it the good stuff. Look for something farm fresh from a local producer.*

Honey Milk

ingredients

- 1½ CUPS WHOLE MILK
- 2 TABLESPOONS MEADOWFOAM HONEY OR OTHER FLAVORFUL HONEY, SUCH AS LAVENDER
- FRESH WHOOP (PAGE 139) FOR GARNISH
- FLEUR DE SEL FOR GARNISH

Whenever I couldn't sleep, had a bad dream, or just needed a little TLC, my mom would make me honey milk. It's exactly what it sounds like—warm milk sweetened with a little honey—and it's just the thing to soothe a worried soul. Turns out I'm not the only one who grew up sipping this comforting blend. I put it on my cart menu and ended up bonding with dozens of customers who grew up with honey milk, too. My version uses rich, full-fat, farm-fresh milk and local meadowfoam honey, which has an amazing vanilla-like flavor with marshmallowy undertones. I top it with fresh whipped cream and a sprinkle of fleur de sel (of course), and dole it out to a steady stream of chilly, rain-soaked Portlanders looking for a steaming mug of comfort.

MAKES 1 SERVING

instructions

- **IN A SMALL NONREACTIVE SAUCEPAN,** heat the milk over medium heat until steaming. Stir in the honey until thoroughly incorporated.
- **POUR INTO A LARGE MUG** and top with whoop and a light sprinkle of fleur de sel.

ingredients

- 1¼ CUPS FROZEN SLICED PEACHES
- 1 CUP FRESH CARROT JUICE (AVAILABLE AT HEALTH FOOD STORES AND TRADER JOE'S)
- 2 TABLESPOONS PLAIN, WHOLE-MILK GREEK YOGURT
- 1 TABLESPOON PLUS 1½ TEASPOONS FLAVORFUL HONEY
- 1½ TEASPOONS PEELED AND GRATED FRESH GINGER

Beta Believe It!

SMOOTHIE

I'm surrounded by sweets all day, so I welcome any opportunity to get a serving of vegetables into my body. That's why I love this smoothie. It's got a healthful dose of beta-carotene–rich carrot juice sweetened with honey and punched up with a little tartness from yogurt and peaches. A bit of fresh ginger adds a refreshing tinge of sweet heat. **MAKES TWO 8-OUNCE SERVINGS**

instructions

- **IN THE BOWL OF A BLENDER,** combine the peaches, carrot juice, yogurt, honey, and ginger and purée until smooth. Divide between two glasses and serve.

ingredients

- 1 CUP FROZEN SLICED PEACHES
- 3/4 CUP (ABOUT 6 OUNCES) SMALL- TO MEDIUM-SIZE FROZEN STRAWBERRIES
- 1 CUP FRESH ORANGE JUICE
- 2 HEAPING TABLESPOONS PLAIN, WHOLE-MILK GREEK YOGURT
- 1 TABLESPOON PLUS 1 1/2 TEASPOONS FLAVORFUL HONEY
- 2 TEASPOONS PEELED AND FRESHLY GRATED GINGER

Teaches of Peaches

SMOOTHIE

This is a favorite at the cart during the hot summer months. It's cold, refreshing, and a little bit sweet, with a touch of heat from the fresh ginger. You can omit the ginger or add less, if you like, but I find that 2 teaspoons is the perfect amount and not at all overwhelming. Remember, ginger is good for you! **MAKES TWO 8-OUNCE SERVINGS**

instructions

- **IN THE BOWL OF A BLENDER,** combine the peaches, strawberries, orange juice, yogurt, honey, and ginger and purée until smooth. Divide between two glasses and serve.

TIP
- *Frozen fruit means you don't need to use ice cubes to achieve that slushy thick texture we love about smoothies. Do your best to seek out organic fruit—especially the strawberries, which soak up pesticides like a sponge, and are one of the most heavily sprayed crops.*

7

SWEET
STAPLES

Sauces, curds, preserves, and frostings—these components can take a dessert from simple to sublime. They can transform a humble cookie into a divine treat, or take a rich, decadent panna cotta and lift it right over the top. This chapter is a collection of my most-used, most-loved components, recipes I always have on hand and use over and over again. They're super easy to make and extremely versatile, and they're a constant source of inspiration as I dream up new ways to share the sugar love.

ingredients

- 12 OUNCES CHOPPED GOOD-QUALITY BITTERSWEET CHOCOLATE
- 14 TABLESPOONS (1³/₄ STICKS) UNSALTED BUTTER, CUT INTO CUBES
- ¹/₄ TEASPOON GOOD SEA SALT, SUCH AS FLEUR DE SEL
- ¹/₄ CUP LIGHT CORN SYRUP

SEXY BITTERSWEET

Chocolate Ganache

This ganache recipe is like a little black dress: It goes with just about anything. Use it as a shiny glaze for cakes and cupcakes, or let it set a bit and use it as a frosting or filling. The addition of light corn syrup keeps the chocolate fluid and glossy while it's warm and gives it a lovely sheen, but it will also set like regular ganache when cool. If you can, splurge on high-quality chocolate such as Valrhona or Felchlin; you'll taste the difference. **MAKES ABOUT 2 CUPS**

instructions

- **IN A MEDIUM METAL BOWL,** combine the chocolate, butter, salt, and corn syrup. Put the bowl over a pan of barely simmering water and heat, stirring, until the chocolate and butter have melted. Remove from the heat.

- **USE AS A GLAZE** for cakes, or let cool until spreadable and use as a frosting or filling. Ganache can be refrigerated for 1 week. To gently rewarm, heat it in a microwave on 50 percent power or put it over a saucepan of barely simmering water and give it a good whisking.

TIP

- *I salt everything—even when a recipe doesn't call for it. We all know a little salt goes a long way toward bringing out the flavors in savory ingredients, but it works the same way with sweet stuff, too, like chocolate and caramel.*

- 3 TABLESPOONS PACKED DARK BROWN SUGAR
- 1/4 TEASPOON SEA SALT
- 3 TABLESPOONS DUTCH PROCESS COCOA POWDER
- 1/2 CUP HEAVY CREAM
- 1/4 CUP LIGHT CORN SYRUP
- 1 TEASPOON UNSALTED BUTTER

AUNTI SHIRLEY'S

Chocolate Sauce

Aunti Shirley was a very close friend of my mom's. I still remember her making me ice-cream sundaes when I was a wee thing and topping them with her homemade chocolate sauce. I recently rediscovered just how wonderful it is. It has an intense, almost black hue, with a silky-smooth rather than gloppy texture. The chocolate flavor isn't overpowering, so it goes with just about everything. I've combined Aunti Shirley's tips with some of my own to make this very versatile topping. Try it on ice cream, of course, and use it to add welcome depth to root beer floats. But you'll also find that it's amazing on Toasted-Coconut Panna Cotta (page 101).

MAKES ABOUT 1 CUP

instructions

- **IN A SMALL SAUCEPAN,** combine the brown sugar, salt, and cocoa powder. Stir in enough heavy cream, a little at a time, to make a paste, and then stir in the remainder. Add the corn syrup and bring to a boil over medium-high heat, making sure to whisk continuously. Reduce the heat to a simmer and continue to cook, whisking continuously, for another 3 to 4 minutes to help cook out the bitter flavor from the cocoa and thicken the sauce. The sauce will be very glossy and take on a very dark hue (almost black).

- **TO TEST IF THE SAUCE IS THICK ENOUGH,** place a small dab of sauce on a clean plate and let stand for 1 minute. If the sauce spreads, keep simmering. You should be able to tip the plate without the sauce running.

- **ONCE DONE,** remove from the heat and stir in the butter. Serve immediately over ice cream or let cool slightly before using. The sauce will keep in an airtight container in the refrigerator for up to 2 weeks. To reheat, microwave at 50 percent power for about 30 seconds, or warm in a saucepan on low heat.

ingredients

- 2 CUPS SUGAR
- 1 CUP WATER
- 1½ TEASPOONS FLEUR DE SEL
- 2 CUPS HEAVY CREAM, WARMED (SEE TIP)
- 1½ TEASPOONS PURE VANILLA EXTRACT

TIPS

- *Warming the cream separately helps to keep the caramel from shocking into a hard mass when you add it. Be sure to add it quickly because you need to stop the cooking process as soon as the caramel turns the color you want. Otherwise, it'll keep cooking, and it can go from perfect to burnt in just a few seconds. If you ever find yourself making caramel and not adding any butter and cream to it, keep a bowl of ice water nearby. Dip the bottom of the pot in the water as soon as the caramel is ready to stop the cooking process.*

- *Be sure the pot is heavy bottomed to promote even cooking, deep enough to hold the caramel when it bubbles up, and light colored (such as stainless steel) so you can see the color of the caramel as it's cooking. When mixing in the cream, use heat-proof utensils such as a wooden spoon or silicone spatula.*

- *To ensure that the sugar does not crystallize, you can add a very small amount of fresh lemon juice (from ½ lemon) to the sugar mixture before putting it on the heat.*

SALTED

Caramel Sauce

I take my caramel to the razor's edge between deliciously deep and flat-out burnt. That's because the darker the color, the more complex and slightly bitter the flavor, and this bitterness pairs very well with desserts. It can help cut the sweetness of something or heighten the flavors. Lighter caramel is sweeter and less complex, but if you like your caramel that way, just cook it to a lighter color than I do. I've made this recipe hundreds of times, and I never use a thermometer, and you shouldn't either. Just trust your senses. Watch it closely, and be sure not to walk away from it because it can burn very fast. This is an easy recipe, but it needs your attention from start to finish, and all your ingredients should be prepped in advance.

MAKES ABOUT 2½ CUPS

instructions

- **IN A DEEP HEAVY-BOTTOMED POT,** combine the sugar, water, and salt and stir until well mixed. Cook over high heat until the sugar starts to color around the edges of the pot, swirling the pan to promote even caramelization of the sugar. (Do not stir or the sugar will crystallize, that is, harden.) Continue cooking, swirling occasionally, until the caramel is very dark mahogany in color and lightly smoking (it should be on the verge of burning), 10 to 15 minutes.

- **IMMEDIATELY REMOVE THE POT** from the heat, and while stirring with a whisk or wooden spoon, add the warmed cream in a steady stream. (Since you're taking the caramel to the dark side, you have to work quickly and begin adding the cream right away to stop the cooking process. But you don't want to add it all at once, so pour it in a continuous, steady stream. Be careful: The mixture will steam and bubble up furiously. I recommend wearing an oven mitt on the hand that's stirring in the cream.) Strain through a fine-mesh sieve into a metal bowl. Stir in the vanilla and let cool at room temperature, stirring occasionally, for about 1 hour. Refrigerate, uncovered, for several hours to thicken.

- **WHISK BEFORE USING** or transferring to an airtight jar for longer storage. It will keep refrigerated for at least 1 week.

ingredients

- 4 LARGE EGGS, AT ROOM TEMPERATURE
- 4 LARGE EGG YOLKS, AT ROOM TEMPERATURE
- 1 CUP SUGAR
- GRATED ZEST OF 2 LEMONS
- 1/2 CUP FRESHLY SQUEEZED LEMON JUICE (FROM ABOUT 4 LEMONS)
- 1/8 TEASPOON SEA SALT
- 1 CUP (2 STICKS) UNSALTED BUTTER, CUT INTO CHUNKS

LUSCIOUS
Lemon Curd

This is hands-down the best lemon curd *and* a serious workhorse. Use it to top cupcakes, scones, or cheesecake; spoon it over shortcakes; or fold it into vanilla ice cream and sandwich between gingersnap cookies. It's creamy, dreamy, lemony goodness. **MAKES 2 CUPS**

instructions

- **IN A MEDIUM STAINLESS-STEEL SAUCEPAN** (don't use aluminum, copper, or cast iron, or it will react with the acidic lemon juice and impart a metallic taste), combine the eggs, egg yolks, sugar, lemon zest, lemon juice, salt, and butter. Cook over medium-low heat, whisking continuously, until the mixture starts to thicken and bubble, about 10 minutes. Remove from the heat and strain through a fine-mesh sieve into a stainless steel bowl.

- **MAKE AN ICE BATH** in a larger bowl and lower the bowl of lemon curd into the bath to stop the cooking process. When the curd has cooled a bit, place plastic wrap directly on the surface to keep it from forming a skin. To help speed up the cooling and thickening process, place the curd—ice bath and all—in the refrigerator.

- **ONCE THE CURD** has completely cooled and thickened, transfer it to an airtight container (or a mason jar, if you want to give some as a gift) and refrigerate for up to 1 week.

VARIATION:

- **THE COOL THING ABOUT THIS RECIPE** is that you don't have to use lemon—you can use whatever potent juice you like. Every once in a while I like to change things up and make The Passion of the Curd (with 3/4 to 1 cup passion fruit purée), Orange Curd, or Lemorange Curd (half lemon and half orange juice).

TIP
- *I know most lemon curd recipes call for a double boiler, but I never make it that way. As long as you whisk constantly and keep the heat moderate, it won't curdle. I like to have a small spoon nearby to dip into the curd while it's cooking and check the texture. If it's running off the spoon I know it needs more time.*

- 12 OUNCES CREAM CHEESE, SOFTENED (I PREFER PHILADELPHIA; SEE TIP)
- 3/4 CUP (1 1/2 STICKS) UNSALTED BUTTER, AT ROOM TEMPERATURE
- 1 CUP CONFECTIONERS' SUGAR, SIFTED
- 1/4 TEASPOON SEA SALT, PLUS MORE TO TASTE (OPTIONAL)
- 1 TEASPOON PURE VANILLA EXTRACT, PLUS MORE TO TASTE (OPTIONAL) (OR MAKE IT FANCY WITH SEEDS FROM 1/2 VANILLA BEAN)

Cream Cheese

FROSTING

If this recipe ends up making more than you need, you could cut it in half, but then you wouldn't have any left over to smear on your toast with jam, or on biscuits or on graham crackers, or to just lick off a spoon. If you ask me, extra frosting is never a bad thing. **MAKES 2 1/2 CUPS**

instructions

- **IN THE BOWL OF A STAND MIXER** fitted with a paddle attachment or in a medium bowl using a handheld mixer, beat the cream cheese and butter until smooth. Scrape down the sides of the bowl. Add the confectioners' sugar, salt, and vanilla and beat until fluffy. Taste and add more salt or vanilla (if desired).

VARIATIONS:

Maple Cream Cheese Frosting

- **ADD** 3 to 4 tablespoons grade B maple syrup along with the vanilla.

Spiced Cream Cheese Frosting

- **ADD** about 1/2 to 1 teaspoon ground cinnamon or 1/4 to 1/2 teaspoon ground cardamom, plus more if desired. Just start small and taste before adding more.

TIP
- *This is frosting, not diet food; so don't go reaching for low-fat cream cheese. Full fat = full flavor. That being said, you don't want to use fancy cream cheese for this. There's something about Philly that makes it just the right texture, flavor, and moistness for baking. Be sure the cheese is softened before using, or else you'll get lumps that are a pain in the butt to beat out. But don't go too far; if the butter and cream cheese are too soft, your frosting will be runny.*

ingredients

- 6 CUPS CHOPPED FRESH OR FROZEN RHUBARB (1/2- TO 1-INCH PIECES; SEE TIP)
- 1 3/4 CUPS SUGAR
- 1/2 TEASPOON SEA SALT
- ZEST AND JUICE OF 1 LEMON (2 TO 3 TABLESPOONS JUICE)
- 1 VANILLA BEAN

Rhubarb Jam

Rhubarb is one of my all-time favorite flavors, so I love using it any chance I get. An easy way for me to work it into my desserts (and my breakfast and lunch) is to turn it into jam. It's so easy to make and much more flavorful and fresh tasting than store-bought. Use it to top scones (see page 31), biscuits (see page 27), vanilla panna cotta (see page 98), and sweet risotto (see page 92). Or make the ultimate ice-cream sandwich: Split a slightly warm glazed buttermilk bar in half horizontally, slather the bottom half with jam, place a couple scoops of ice cream on top—Cream Soda Ice Cream (page 107), vanilla bean, or ginger are all awesome—and then replace the top. Come summertime, this is a serious customer favorite. Clearly there's no end to this jam's uses. The vanilla bean rounds out the flavor and adds lovely specks, so don't skip it. The jam keeps in the refrigerator for several weeks, or you can process it in a boiling-water canner for longer storage.

MAKES ABOUT 3 CUPS

instructions

- **IN A MEDIUM HEAVY-BOTTOMED SAUCEPAN,** combine the rhubarb, sugar, salt, and lemon zest and juice. Split the vanilla bean lengthwise and scrape out the seeds with the back of a knife. Add to the pan along with the pod and bring to a boil over medium heat. Cook, stirring occasionally, until the rhubarb is tender and the mixture has thickened, 15 to 20 minutes.

- **REMOVE FROM THE HEAT** and let cool before transferring the mixture to an airtight container and refrigerating.

TIP
- *When shopping for fresh rhubarb, choose the stalks with the darkest red color; they'll impart the best color, and, in my opinion, they also have a better flavor.*

- 2 TABLESPOONS BUTTERMILK OR PLAIN YOGURT WITH LIVE CULTURES
- 2 CUPS HEAVY CREAM (NOT ULTRA-PASTEURIZED)

DIY

Crème Fraîche

Do you really need to spend $5 on a 4-ounce tub of crème fraîche? No, not when you can easily make it yourself for half the price. It's really just cream that's been colonized by good bacteria, which you can duplicate by mixing cream with a cultured dairy product like buttermilk or yogurt and letting it sit in a warm place to encourage those good little bugs to get busy. Crème fraîche is great when lightened with whipped cream and used as a topping for pies and tarts or as a filling for cakes like the Badonkadonk Shortcake (page 82). Think of it as fancy sour cream. In summertime, when the air is warm, it's effortless to whip up. In cooler months, you may need to experiment to find a warm enough place to keep it. Try leaving it on top of a stove with a pilot light, a heating pad, a water heater, or a radiator. **MAKES ABOUT 2 CUPS**

instructions

- **IN A SMALL NONREACTIVE BOWL,** whisk together the buttermilk and cream. Pour the mixture into a clean glass jar, place the lid slightly ajar, and leave in a warm place (at least 70°F) until slightly thickened, at least 8 and up to 24 hours. Stir, then cover and chill until thickened a bit more. It will keep in an airtight container for up to 2 weeks.

TIP

- *If the cream doesn't thicken within 24 hours of sitting out somewhere warm, toss it. There are several likely scenarios to explain what happened: Your buttermilk or yogurt didn't have any live cultures, your cream was ultra-pasteurized, or the mixture got too hot and killed the bacteria.*

Fresh Whoop

At the cart, just about everything gets a hit of Fresh Whoop (Southern slang for "whipped cream"). I can't help it. Everything tastes better with whipped cream. Besides, it's what my mom always did. She was obsessed with the stuff and passed that trait right on to me. She never used the stuff in the canister or Cool Whip because they don't count. Fresh whipped cream is just that—fresh cream whipped right on the spot. It tastes so much better than any of the commercial pretenders. Plus, it's a blank canvas, so you can flavor it dozens of different ways. When I want to add depth, I use dark brown sugar instead of granulated. When I want to get boozy, I use spirits or liqueurs. You can also add a pinch or two of ground spices, or infuse the cream with herbs or whole spices: Heat the cream with them, allow to steep until it tastes the way you like it, then strain and chill before whipping.

MAKES ABOUT 2 CUPS

instructions

- **IN THE BOWL OF A STAND MIXER** fitted with a whisk attachment, combine the cream, sugar, and vanilla and beat on medium-high speed until medium-soft peaks form. (Alternatively you can whip the cream with a handheld mixer or by hand with a whisk, though it'll take a longer.) If you want the peaks softer, whip less. If you want them sturdier, whip longer, but don't overwhip or the cream will curdle and eventually turn into butter!

VARIATION:

Nutella Whoop

I grew up on Nutella like most other kids grow up on peanut butter. My mom loved the stuff (she pronounced it "NEW-tell-a"), and I swear she put it on everything. Now I do, too. One of my favorites is whipping it into fresh cream for a most decadent chocolate-hazelnut whoop. It's amazing on my Milk Chocolate Pôts de Crème (page 95), but I'm sure you can find dozens of other uses, too.

- **FOLLOW THE PRECEDING RECIPE,** but before you whip the cream, add 3 to 4 tablespoons of room-temperature Nutella to the bowl. Whip until medium-soft peaks form.

index